Endorsements

The Blood of Jesus is truly the most important subject and truth in Scripture. It is the very essence of our salvation, and I believe it deserves our full attention! As you spend time in this 31-day devotional, *His Blood Speaks* will help you build your faith daily by reading and meditating on what Jesus accomplished for you through His precious Blood. It is a must-have for every library!

—**Pastors Hank** and **Brenda Kunneman**
Lord Of Hosts Church and One Voice Ministries
Omaha, NE

Messages concerning the Blood of Jesus are rare in this time of the Church. Even though the message of the Blood seems to be rare, it is anything but rare. The Blood might not be spoken in the language of men, but it is a constant subject being spoken of in Spirit language. However, the full aspect of faith is man's spirit and soul and body to be in agreement with the Truth that sets men free. This book is likened to the interpretation of the language of the Spirit so that man's spirit, soul, and body can cooperate with God's Truth.

I perceive that this subject and book will become a daily part of the believer's devotion. Reading this book has awakened a deep hunger in me to constantly believe, think, and speak in what the Blood of Jesus Christ has done and is still doing for me. What a timely devotion and an excellent layout of teaching concerning the power of the Blood of Jesus.

—**Fred Brothers**
Faith Christian Fellowship
Tulsa, OK

I have known Ginger for more than 18 years as a friend and mentor. She is the first person I turn to when I need solid Biblical wisdom or advice. She has an amazing gift for the prophetic, as well as being one of the greatest prayer warriors I know of. I can honestly say when she prays, all of heaven stops to listen. Her gifts and strengths are not just God-given but have been tried in the fires of personal victory time and time again! She knows what spiritual warfare looks, smells, and feels like. When there is a battle at hand, no matter how big, she runs straight toward it with sword and shield at the ready. Ginger is one of the rarest of believers who easily demonstrates what it means to be called a child after God's own heart! I am truly blessed and honored to be called her friend.

—**Jeremy Silbernagel**
Associate Pastor, Gateway Church
Southlake, TX

Powerful and life changing! The Blood of Jesus Christ is the weapon that will empower you to live a victorious life in Christ!

—**Pastor Trudy Eusebi**
Trudy Eusebi Ministries
Costa Mesa, CA

The insight the Lord has given Ginger on the Blood of Jesus is powerful! I wished I had known this years ago! There is power in the Name and Blood of Jesus! Thank you, Ginger!

—**Paul Hutton**
Hutton Financial Advisors
Weatherford, TX

There are so many voices in the world, but there is nothing more powerful than the perpetual, powerful voice of the Blood of Jesus. As you digest the words of this devotional on a daily basis, you will begin to hear the voice of Jesus' Blood cry out—honor instead of shame, innocence instead of guilt, righteousness instead of unrighteousness, freedom instead of addiction, exoneration instead of condemnation, approval instead of disapproval, health and wholeness instead of sickness and disease, prosperity and blessing instead of poverty and lack, worthiness instead of unworthiness, acceptance instead of rejection, and the list goes on.

Ginger Ziegler (my mom) so eloquently unpacks and unfolds the Scriptures and reveals outstanding treasures found in the Word of God pertaining to Jesus' Blood continuously speaking on your behalf. The confession and prayer at the end of each day activate what you've read. It is sure to open the door to freedom from things that have plagued you and many believers for generations.

This is one of the most significant and influential books written. It's a must read—again and again! Your freedom lies within the pages of this daily devotional.

—**Michael** and **Sherrie Howell**
The New Sound Is Family
Fort Worth, TX

HIS BLOOD

Harrison House

Shippensburg, PA

31-DAY DEVOTIONAL

HIS BLOOD

Speaks

YOUR VICTORY—
THE DEVIL'S DEFEAT

GINGER ZIEGLER

Published by Harrison House Publishers
Shippensburg, PA 17257

ISBN 13 TP: 978-1-6803-1984-2

ISBN 13 eBook: 978-1-6803-1985-9

For Worldwide Distribution, Printed in the U.S.A.

1 2 3 4 5 6 7 8 / 26 25 24 23 22

Dedication

To my awesome family who has stood by me in honor
and love—the depth of my love for you is indescrib-
able and goes beyond words.

To my amazing prayer partners who prayed
through the storms, shouted victory, and held me in
your continual prayers with your dedication and commitment—my heart overflows with gratitude.

Most of all, to my Lord Jesus Christ—our friend-
ship is the sweetest! You have dealt with me mercifully
and crowned me with Your Grace! You have dried every tear, made me laugh, picked me up, held my hand,
and always stayed by my side. All the special "secret"
things You have done constantly reveal Your love,
keeping me encouraged through my journey of faith.
Thank *You!* I am forever grateful.

Contents

Foreword

SECOND Corinthians 10:4 tells us that the weapons of our warfare are *mighty* through God for the dismantling of enemy strongholds. We have weapons because the warfare that satan launched against mankind in the garden still exists. God has given us weapons that Jesus proved to be more powerful than the combined efforts of all spiritual and natural forces. The challenge we have is not in the weapons we've been given, but in how to use them effectively. But in these end-time days, the Church cannot afford to be hampered by such ignorance. Too much is at stake.

While our weapons are many, the greatest of them are the Word of God, His Wonderful Name, and the Precious Blood of Jesus. Sadly, we know far too little about the power in His Blood. This lack of knowledge has handicapped the Church for most of its existence.

Thankfully, Ginger has given us a way to daily learn from the Word about the power that's in the Blood and how to apply it. The Blood as a weapon has been a major part of her life's focus. But it's her amazing prayer life that testifies of her skill in using this most powerful weapon. We are privileged to glean from her knowledge and experience in the brilliant format of a daily devotional. You will find yourself chewing on the bite-size revelations all day long.

Yet perhaps the greatest benefit is the unseen blessing of having Ginger's prayers activated on your behalf, for I have no doubt she has prayed and is praying over every reader. That along with the revelation knowledge on each page is worth far more than the price of the book or the time it takes to read it. Praise God and thank you, Ginger, for this treasure. It is marvelous in our eyes!

—**Pastor Terri Copeland Pearsons**
Kenneth Copeland Ministries
Eagle Mountain International Church
Fort Worth, Texas

Preface

IN the early '90s the Lord showed me that in my latter years, hardships and difficulties would transpire not only in our nation but throughout the world. I wanted to publish a book that would help my precious family, as well as others, stand strong in the Lord.

It's my desire that this devotional impact readers in such a way that they are enabled to do exploits for the Lord and be fully equipped to fulfill God's will in these last days.

The writing of this book has been a very long journey. I first heard a series of messages in the late '80s on *The Blood Speaks*. The words from those sermons went deep into my heart. It was almost as if I memorized each word that was spoken because they were so real to me. After hearing about the power of the Blood through those sermons, as I traveled to different nations ministering, this was my main message during those years.

When I began this ministry in 1991, the Lord asked me to write a daily devotional on what I had learned and experienced during the prior years. Now, don't laugh when I tell you this story. I wrote the words to this book. Then I printed them out on an old dot matrix printer. I carefully cut each page and used staples and tape to "make my book." I stuck it in my back pocket and said, "Lord, tell me when to print it." Ha! So, I've carried this book around a long time! It's time for it to be birthed because nations of people need this daily weapon to win!

While I was ministering in Cape Town, South Africa in the early '90s, the Lord revealed things which would eventually take place in our nation. He asked me to conduct prayer meetings where He would give us the ability to "hold back the sun and moon" like Joshua did to spare our nation from impending danger. I did just that. We've held untold prayer meetings for our nation. During those years, He also showed me how this book would be a help and blessing to many by teaching them how to stand strong against the devices of the devil in the coming days.

Has this been easy? No! I've fought many battles, alongside my prayer partners, to see this book come to fruition. The warfare has been tremendous, to put it mildly. The devil certainly didn't want people to have this weapon in their hands. Through the years, it has been edited and refined while waiting for such a time as this. That time is now. I know this daily devotional will help you stand strong and "win" in this lifetime!

May God's richest blessings of revelation and insight come to you continually as you pray, study His Word, and make your decrees.

Blessings in abundance and beyond,
Ginger

Introduction

THE truth about the Blood of Jesus speaking is one of the most powerful revelations you can receive from the Lord. It can mean the difference between life or death, victory or defeat, in every area of your life.

Like a roaring lion, the devil is roaming around seeking whom he may devour (1 Peter 5:8). He has been overcome by the power of Jesus' Blood and the word of your testimony. To enforce that authority and power effectively, you must understand the Blood of Jesus is not simply a silent, historical fact. The Blood of Jesus has the power to overcome anything and everything including satan himself on your behalf!

His Blood is a living reality. Every day the Blood of Jesus is speaking continually to you and for you. It truly is the Blood of sprinkling that speaks (1 Peter 1:2; Hebrews 12:24)! The revelation about what the Blood is saying has been helping God's people live as overcomers for more than 2,000 years. In recent times, the emphasis on the Blood of Jesus hasn't been as major as other teachings.

The Blood of Jesus is the foundation on which Christianity is based. Christians at times saw the Blood of Jesus primarily from an emotional perspective. The thought of it does little more than stir deep feelings within and remind them of the passion of Jesus on the cross. Such sentiments are precious as far as they go, but they don't go far enough.

The Blood of Jesus is more than an emotion-filled memory! It is the major weapon for everyday living. It's powerful and unique in its ability to rescue. It's absolutely effective in enforcing satan's defeat.

Years ago, I received a mandate from God: "Prepare My people for the days ahead through a daily study of the power in the Blood of Jesus." This book is my response to Him.

It was written with you in mind. Its purpose is to provide you with life-altering insights into the treasury of the riches of the glory of God's Grace, and to help you behold what has been provided for you through the shed Blood of our beloved Savior, Jesus Christ.

The daily devotional format is designed to fit into your busy schedule so you can conveniently and immediately put into practice what you learn.

To receive maximum benefit, you should consider reading this book out loud every day. Say each word slowly and thoughtfully. Believing always leads to speaking as it's the inevitable progression of faith. As you speak out loud what you believe, these truths will be reinforced, because faith comes by hearing and understanding the Word of God (Romans 10:17).

Jesus' Blood is the change agent. Speaking what the Word of God says will cause a very real change to take place inside you. You'll be permanently transformed from the inside out as you agree with the Word and with the Blood. Your potential in life will explode exponentially as you read and speak these truths over and over again.

Before you begin, determine in your heart to lay hold of the fact that the Blood is speaking for you and to you. Set your sights on getting stronger in that revelation each day so that you can use it effectively against the enemy. Satan already understands the legality of his defeat by the power of the Blood of Jesus. Once you fully understand it too, you'll be able to triumph legally against him. You'll be able to overcome even satan himself.

The time has come for all of us in the Church of Jesus Christ to stop playing defense in dealing with the devil. It's time for us to go on the offense! We can live in a continual place of victory over every onslaught of the enemy by acknowledging the victory that Jesus has already given us through the power of His Blood and His Name.

This is the day of the overcomer!

This is your time of victory!

Ginger

Day 1

His Blood Speaks...Now

But you have come to Mount Zion and to the city of the living God, the heavenly Jerusalem, to an innumerable company of angels, to the general assembly and church of the firstborn who are registered in heaven, to God the Judge of all, to the spirits of just men made perfect, to Jesus the Mediator of the new covenant, and to the blood of sprinkling that speaks better things than that of Abel. See that you do not refuse Him who speaks. For if they did not escape who refused Him who spoke on earth, much more shall we not escape if we turn away from Him who speaks from heaven.

—Hebrews 12:22-25 NKJV

THESE verses from Hebrews provide the foundation for this entire book. They will encourage you causing your soul to prosper as you meditate on them. First, notice that they say that *right now*, in the present tense, "You have come to Jesus." You are no longer separated from Him. Jesus has brought you to Himself through His Blood. The Blood gives you free access to Him at this very moment. It provides you with confident, immediate entrance into His Presence—*now!*

Also notice these verses say that the Blood "speaks." That might sound strange to your natural mind, yet the Bible says it's true.

How can *blood* speak?

It's living tissue. *"The life of the flesh is in the blood"* (Leviticus 17:11). Blood can speak because it has life in it.

The first Scriptural record we have of blood speaking is in Genesis when Adam and Eve's son, Abel, was murdered by his brother, Cain. Genesis 4:3-10 says after Abel was killed, his blood spoke from the ground and told the Lord something. It cried "vengeance!" Think about that. Abel's blood had a voice. It actually talked and God heard what it said.

Now consider this: The Blood of Jesus is talking too!

As a believer, you have come to that Blood—the Blood of sprinkling that speaks *better* things than that of Abel. *Better* is a key word in the book of Hebrews. It appears there 12 times. It refers to something that is stronger, superior, more excellent, and nobler.

It's wonderful to know the Blood of Jesus is saying better things about you. His Blood says Mercy!

Instead of crying out for vengeance like Abel's blood, Jesus' Blood cries for mercy, forgiveness, restoration, health, pardon, justification, peace, cleansing, reconciliation, redemption, protection, eternal covenant, overcoming victory, and everything else you will ever need now and throughout eternity. Glory to God!

Here are some of the things the Blood has to say about you right now that you can agree with concerning your life:

+ I am not guilty. There is no case pending against me in Heaven's court.

+ I am redeemed, bought back, paid for in full.

+ I am forgiven, just like I never sinned.

+ I am washed clean, inside and out.

+ I am justified and innocent, not guilty.

+ I am reconciled to my Heavenly Father.

+ I am sanctified, made holy.

+ I have peace with God.

+ I can fulfill His plan for my life. My destiny and purpose are intact.

+ I am able to approach God with free access to ask for anything I want or need in accordance with His will and His Word.

+ I have a covenant that is eternal. It lasts forever.

+ I am protected.

+ I am healed.

+ I am prosperous.

+ I am a vessel for His Glory.

+ I am a victorious overcomer, even over satan himself.

Grab hold of this by faith now—because faith is always now—*right now!* You can come to Jesus at this very moment and experience the delivering power His Blood provides. His Blood is speaking all these things for you *now* (Hebrews 11:1).

This is the truth! Jesus' Blood has a voice. It's the Voice of Mercy. It speaks of the Covenant of Mercy. It's declaring that Covenant *for* you and *to* you now.

Listen! Can you hear His Voice through His Blood?

Listen with your heart. His Blood is talking *to* you and *for* you. Close your eyes and speak what the Blood is saying.

Can you see it? Can you hear His Blood? Can you hear His Voice speaking to you?

Let it paint a picture inside. Believe what He's saying. Receive all the Blood has done and is doing for you at this very moment. Embrace this: Jesus' Blood is speaking loudly *to* me and *for* me.

Prayer and Confession

Heavenly Father, today I have come to Jesus, Your Son. This day, at this moment, I am in the presence of His Blood and it's speaking now. It's preaching a noble, more excellent, superior message—a message of mercy which all of the realms of existence can hear.

*Jesus, thank You for the life that is given to me through Your Blood, because the life is in the blood. I know Your very own life is speaking **for** me, **to** me, and **on** my behalf.*

I proclaim Your Blood by faith today for my family, friends, loved ones, our nation, and myself. I set myself in agreement with the witness of the Spirit, the Word, and the Blood, because they agree that Jesus is Lord! They agree that I can overcome anything and everything by Your Blood. I am victorious through Jesus' Blood. He has made a way for me where there seems to be no way. I've found the way of life through Your Blood.

*Thank You, Father. Thank You, Jesus. Thank You, Holy Spirit. Father, I know my prayer is being heard and answered because You always hear what the Blood of Jesus has to say on my behalf. In Jesus' Name, I pray and believe I receive now—**today, at this moment**—all that the Blood has to offer to me and my family!*

Proclaim and Decree

I am redeemed. I am forgiven. I am reconciled to my Heavenly Father.

Other Scriptures to Study

Exodus 12:7

Hebrews 9:19

Hebrews 11:24-29

Day 2

His Blood Speaks Better Things

By faith Abel offered to God a more excellent sacrifice than Cain, through which he obtained witness that he was righteous, God testifying of his gifts; and through it he being dead still speaks.

—Hebrews 11:4 NKJV

IN the story of Cain and Abel, the conflict began when each of the brothers brought God an offering. Abel sacrificed to Him the firstborn of his flock. Cain brought Him fruit from his crops. Those two offerings might seem much the same from our perspective, but not from God's.

He accepted Abel's gift and rejected Cain's. Why?

The answer has everything to do with the blood.

"The wages of sin is death" (Romans 6:23). It takes a blood payment to satisfy divine justice when sin has been committed. Both Cain and Abel knew this was true. Their parents, Adam and Eve, tried to use fig leaves to cover their sin when they disobeyed God in the Garden of Eden. The leaves were insufficient. So, God shed

the blood of an animal to cover their transgressions. Then He used the skin of the animals to make their clothes (Genesis 3:7-21).

From that time on in the Old Testament, God required the blood of animals to atone for sin. Yet Cain brought God a non-blood sacrifice. Resorting to a form of religion, he tried to offer what was comfortable instead of what God required. His offering was just a matter of ritual, without meaning or life, without commitment, and without obedience.

Abel did things God's way. He went to the Lord by faith with his sacrifice of blood, recognizing his sinfulness and his need for God's mercy. God accepted his gift. He testified that it was pleasing to Him. By that gift Abel obtained the witness that he was righteous.

If you're wondering now what this story has to do with you, I'll tell you!

Like Abel, you have obtained the witness that you are righteous—not because of an Old Testament sacrifice, but by and through the Blood of Jesus. Because Jesus was made sin in your place, His Blood declares you have been made right on the inside and right in your relationship with the Father (2 Corinthians 5:21). It testifies that you are being conformed and renewed to the image of Christ on a daily basis (Romans 8:29).

The testimony of His Blood isn't just a quiet whisper either, but a thunderous declaration! It's making the same kind of loud proclamation Abel's blood made *but* proclaims Mercy!

In the midst of Cain's jealous rage over his offering being rejected, he killed his brother and tried to cover up the murder by telling God he didn't know where Abel was. But the voice of Abel's blood contradicted him.

"What have you done?" God said to Cain. *"The voice of your brother's blood cries out to Me from the ground"* (Genesis 4:10 NKJV).

Notice, God said He could hear Abel's blood *crying*. The word *cry* can mean to shriek, call out, or to proclaim. *Proclaim* can mean to declare publicly where everyone can hear it. Abel's blood called out in a shrieking voice, making a public proclamation before God and man that his life had been poured out into the ground in anger, jealousy, and wrath.

Abel's blood had a booming voice. It was the voice of vengeance wanting justice. Hebrews 11:4 says, *"He being dead yet speaks."*

Thankfully, Jesus' Blood is speaking too—and with an even stronger Voice! But instead of vengeance, His blood speaks *Mercy*. His Blood says *to* you, "God is not mad at you!" His Blood says *for* you, "Father, have mercy on them because I love them." Jesus' Blood didn't cry out for Himself. It cried out for *you!*

Even 2,000 years after His Blood was shed on the cross, it still *"speaks better things than that of Abel"* (Hebrews 12:24 NKJV).

The Greek word translated *speaks* can mean to talk, utter words, preach, say, speak, and tell. In the Gospels it's used to refer to Jesus speaking and can be translated as speak, spake, spoken, and told more than 100 times. Several times it refers to the Holy Ghost speaking.

The root of this Greek word can mean to break silence. When Abel's blood cried out, it shrieked and proclaimed that a wrong had been done.

Abel's blood broke Cain's silence and revealed his sin. Jesus' Blood does just the opposite. His Blood breaks the silence and removes sin! It declares that our Covenant with God has been restored.

The Blood of Jesus has purpose. Within the purpose is the message of God's desire for a family. It cries forgiveness and mercy, not judgment.

Oh, what good news that is! The silence of the ages has been broken! The Father hears the Blood of Jesus speaking on behalf of mankind, not against mankind. The devil thought he had silenced Jesus when he killed Him. But when the last drop of Jesus' life force drained out of Him, the Voice of His Blood began to fill the earth, the heavens...and even hell itself.

Even satan himself couldn't silence the Blood of Jesus and still can't!

Today, that Blood is speaking better things. It's speaking excellent, superior things about you and to you. It's proclaiming mercy, mercy, and more mercy—and mercy always triumphs over judgment (James 2:13).

Say it out loud now:

"Today, the Blood of Jesus is speaking stronger, more excellent, and superior things *to* me, *for* me, and *about* me! His Blood is declaring mercy over me!"

Prayer and Confession

*Father, I can see that Your pure Life is in the Blood of Jesus. His Blood is Anointed. The Anointing in the Blood of Jesus removes burdens and destroys the bondage of the devil in my life (Isaiah 10:27). I accept Him who speaks **to** me and **for** me and **on** my behalf.*

The Blood says things that are more excellent about me right now. I have a better, stronger, nobler Covenant because of the Blood. Jesus, thank You for opening my eyes to see these truths. I am more than an overcomer in all things because of You. I speak the power of Your Blood for my children, grandchildren, and loved ones. It delivers and sets us free. The devil is defeated because of that power! I glorify You, Jesus, because You are Lord!

Proclaim and Decree

I am the righteousness of God, because the Blood of Jesus speaks mercy.

Other Scriptures to Study

Luke 11:51

Day 3

His Blood Releases
the Power of the Anointing

*It shall come to pass in that day, that his [the enemy's]
burden shall be taken away from off thy shoulder, and his
yoke from off thy neck, and the yoke shall be destroyed
because of the anointing.*

—Isaiah 10:27

WE don't use the word *anointing* much in ordinary conversation these days. But in the Bible, it's a vital word. It refers to the mighty power of the Holy Spirit that operated through Jesus. In fact, the Greek word *Christ* that so often is joined with Jesus' Name in Scripture literally can be translated "the Anointed One and His Anointing" (Luke 4:18-19).

First Peter 1:18-19 tells us we've been redeemed by the "precious Blood of Christ." That preciousness or value of Christ's Blood gives power to His Blood being Anointed for deliverance. That means Jesus' Blood is Anointed with the Holy Spirit's power. Every drop of it is a container of the Anointing.

**It is Anointed Blood...with an Anointed
Voice...and an Anointed message.**

Why is that so important?

Because, according to Isaiah 10:27, the Anointing has the power, authority, and ability to remove all burdens and destroy all yokes. A *yoke* can refer to some type of abuse. A *burden* can mean to drag one's self along.

You know from experience—just as I do—it's a painful thing to suffer abuse. It's terrible to be dragged down by the cares of life. We all want to be free of such things. Thank God, Jesus' Blood makes it possible!

His Blood has the power to remove all burdens from our shoulders! It has the power to destroy all yokes from around our necks (Isaiah 10:27).

The word *destroy* can mean to demolish something to the point where it can *never, ever* be put back together again.

It paints the picture of grinding a yoke into powder.

Think of it! This is what Jesus has done for you. He didn't just break the yokes the devil constructed for you so that they could be repaired later. No! By shedding His Blood, Jesus pulverized those yokes so thoroughly that they ceased to exist. He wiped them out forever!

That was Jesus' mission when He went to the cross. It's the reason He willingly submitted when His persecutors beat Him on His back. He did it so that you would not have to submit to the cares of this life, living loaded down with burdens on your back.

Isaiah 53:4-5,7 says it this way:

Surely he hath borne our griefs, and carried our sorrows...he was wounded for our transgressions, he was bruised for our iniquities: the chastisement of our peace was upon him; and with his stripes we are healed...He was oppressed, and he was afflicted, yet he opened not his mouth.

Look again at that last verse. It says that instead of speaking up for Himself and declaring His innocence, Jesus kept silent. Because of that silence, the devil thought he had triumphed over Jesus once and for all. But he soon found out that when Jesus' mouth was closed,

His Blood cried out!

Now that Blood is speaking a message to the whole universe. It's speaking words of life *to* you and *for* you. The Blood of Jesus has something to tell you and to say about you.

No matter how hard the devil tries, he can't stop that Blood from speaking. He can't stop the Anointing from delivering you. Its power is too great for him. When you receive by faith the power of Jesus' Anointed Blood, together with His Name and the Word of God, nothing can by any means hurt or harm you in any way (Luke 10:19).

The victory has already been won. It's already been settled. Why should you allow the devil to keep abusing you? Why should you keep dragging yourself along life's road? Let the Anointed Blood take all those burdens the devil has tried to place on your back and remove and totally destroy them for you!

It's time to speak the Blood, apply the Anointing, and be free!

The Blood of Jesus already is speaking on your behalf. Its message is eternal. His Blood is telling you, your family, the whole earth, your Heavenly Father, the angels, the devil, and his demons what already has been accomplished. It's declaring that the enemy's yoke has been permanently and totally destroyed!

Hebrews 12:25 warns, *"See that ye refuse not him that speaketh."* We must heed that warning. We must not refuse the message of Jesus' Blood. We must be quick to believe, speak, and act on what that Blood says *to* us, *about* us, and *for* us.

Listen to what the Blood says! It's speaking now.

It speaks words of life. It preaches. It has an Anointed Voice. At this very moment, the Blood is speaking from the Mercy Seat of God in Heaven and saying:

- ◆ You can stop dragging yourself along.
- ◆ You can get all those burdens off you.
- ◆ The Blood and the Anointing can empower you to walk upright, strong, and victorious. You're free!

Prayer and Confession

Heavenly Father, my Father of love and light, thank You for revealing Yourself to me through and by the Blood of Jesus. My life is changing. I can sense the difference inside as I meditate upon the precious Blood. I believe

I am a vessel of honor for Your Glory. I am victorious. I am an overcomer because Your Word is truth. That truth is changing me from the inside out.

Thank You, Jesus. Thank You, Holy Spirit, for teaching me who I am in Christ and who He is in me. My soul is prospering. Therefore, I am prospering and living in health.

*I will not let the devil drag me around and abuse me anymore. I'm letting the Anointing and the Blood speak **to** me and **for** me right now.*

The Blood is speaking for my loved ones right now, even if they don't know it. The Voice that is in the Blood can't be silenced. The devil can't win because of the Blood and Name of Jesus.

Proclaim and Decree

I am free. The Blood and the Anointing are empowering me to walk upright, strong, and victorious.

Other Scriptures to Study

Hebrews 8:6

Hebrews 9:19-28

Hebrews 10:22-23

Day 4

His Blood Is a Witness
to You and for You

*One witness shall not rise against a man concerning any
iniquity or any sin that he commits; by the mouth of two
or three witnesses the matter shall be established.*

—Deuteronomy 19:15 NKJV

IN our courtrooms this happens every day: a defendant stands
before a judge accused of a crime. Their guilt or innocence
hangs in the balance. Either they'll be convicted and punished
or acquitted and set free. The verdict depends on the testimony of
the witnesses.

In the court room of Heaven and on earth, the same scene
unfolds. The devil, acting as prosecutor and accuser of the brethren, brings charges against us (Job 1:6). Our Heavenly Father, the
Judge of all, is presiding over our case. He loves us and wants to
rule in our favor, but divine justice demands that the proper evi-
dence be presented.

**It's a legal battle. It must be won
according to the rules of divine law.**

"Let's call for the witnesses!" says the Judge. "We'll see who's innocent and who's guilty. Bring in the witnesses and let them testify. Only they can shut the accuser's mouth."

In response to His call, the witnesses for our defense take the stand. Who are they? The Bible says it this way:

> This is He who came by water and blood, Jesus Christ; not only by water, but by water and blood. And it is the Spirit who bears witness, because the Spirit is truth. For there are three that bear witness in heaven: the Father, the Word, and the Holy Spirit; and these three are one.
>
> —1 John 5:6-7 NKJV

This is the wonderful defense team God has assembled for us—the Spirit, the Word, and the Blood. All three witnesses are unified in agreement on our behalf. They testify that the guilt of our sin has been borne by another. The price for it has been paid. "This defendant is innocent!" they declare. "There is no legal case against them. They must be set free!"

According to God's legal system, "in the mouth of two or three witnesses shall every word be established" (2 Corinthians 13:1). He declares the matter is settled. As far as He's concerned, we—the accused—have been vindicated. The case is closed! We need to believe that too!

You may say, "But if that's true, why is the devil still giving me trouble? Why does he still harass me day after day?"

Because in your life, one more witness is needed.

The Spirit, the Word, and the Blood already have given their testimony. *Now you must give yours.* For the verdict of Heaven to become a reality for you, you must use your mouth to say the same thing God's three witnesses are saying.

You are the *establishing witness* in your own life!

You have the power to cast down the accusations of satan and overcome him by the Blood of the Lamb and by the word of your testimony (Revelation 12:10-11).

This is how you apply the Blood of Jesus! You do it with your words. You do it by setting yourself in agreement with every Word that Blood speaks *to* you and *for* you.

There's power in agreement. It can either be positive or negative. If you side with the devil and his accusations, your agreement will work against you. If you agree with Jesus and the testimony of His Blood, it will work for you in a powerful way against the devil.

The choice is yours. God has *"set before you life and death, blessing and cursing: therefore choose life"* (Deuteronomy 30:19). Choose to cultivate a greater awareness of the Blood of Jesus speaking. Remind yourself often that His Blood is speaking to God.

It's speaking *for* you and it's speaking *to* you.

It has taken the heavenly witness stand, because Christ came as our High Priest and,

*...with His own Blood He entered the Most Holy Place
once for all, having obtained eternal redemption for us.*

—Hebrews 9:12 NKJV

Picture this in your mind and heart. After His resurrection, Jesus, your High Priest, took His precious Blood into the Holy Place, to the Throne of God in Heaven, and sprinkled it there to secure your sanctification *once and for all.*

As He sprinkled His Blood, it began to speak for you and call your name and it has never stopped.

It still speaks continually for you. It is still testifying today that Jesus has obtained eternal redemption for you.

Forever, His Blood will be speaking for you from the Heavenly Holy Place! Even now, it is talking *to* you and *for* you, saying:

The verdict has been rendered. You have been declared "not guilty" in Jesus' Name. Call your name out loud and say:

I, _____, have been vindicated. My case is closed. It is finished and settled forever for me!

(sign your name) _____

You cannot separate Jesus and His Blood. They are One.

They have witnessed against the enemy on your behalf. They have witnessed to God, the Almighty Judge, on your behalf. He has accepted their witness. The great exchange has been made. The legal battle has been won. Jesus has taken your guilt, and by faith in Him you have received His righteousness.

You now have the power of God on your side. You have His pure life in you and on you today. You have been set completely free through the precious and powerful Blood of the Lamb.

Prayer and Confession

My precious Heavenly Father, I set myself in agreement with Your Word, with the Blood, and with Your Spirit today. Right now, this moment, I believe I have all the Blood has bought for me. I believe Jesus is alive and making intercession for me right now; His Blood speaks mercy for me, my family, and my friends.

I am a witness to what the Blood says. My testimony is what the Blood of Jesus has done, is doing, and will continue to do for me, to me, and with me. Thank You, my Lord and Savior! I have no fear because I can hear Your Blood, Your Word, and Your Spirit speaking to me. It's signed, sealed, and I am delivered:

(sign your name) _____

Proclaim and Decree

I am not guilty. I'm innocent, and there is no case pending.

Other Scriptures to Study

Exodus 19:1-25

Exodus 20:18-21

Numbers 35:30

Hebrews 8:6

The Price Has Been Paid in Full

When Pilate saw that he could prevail nothing, but that rather a tumult was made, he took water, and washed his hands before the multitude, saying, I am innocent of the blood of this just person: see ye to it. Then answered all the people, and said, His blood be on us, and on our children. Then released he Barabbas unto them: and when he had scourged Jesus, he delivered him to be crucified…And they stripped him, and put on him a scarlet robe. And when they had platted a crown of thorns, they put it upon his head…And after that they had mocked him, they took the robe off from him, and put his own raiment on him, and led him away to crucify him.

—Matthew 27:24-26, 28-29, 31

GO back with me to the day they crucified our Lord and Savior. I want you to see what was done to Him. I know it's painful to look at, but faith requires a clear picture.

That's why the Word so graphically portrays Jesus' betrayal and crucifixion. God knows that as believers we must see all that Jesus bore if we are to fully receive the benefits. We can only believe that we don't have to pay any penalty for our sin if we see for ourselves that Jesus paid the whole price. He paid it all for you and me!

Our understanding about what really happened to Him that day has been so undeveloped and limited. We have the idea that the nail holes in His hands were just pinpricks, that only a little bit of blood poured out of His side—a few drops here and there.

But I want you to see the event like it really happened!

Even before Jesus was nailed to the cross, His Blood flowed like rivers. In the Garden, His sweat was as it were great drops of Blood flowing from His head as He submitted to the cross for you and me (Luke 22:44). He was flogged with a whip called a cat-of-nine-tails. It struck His back, wrapped around His body, and ripped His flesh off of Him, separating tissue from bone. With every lash, His Blood splattered the room and splashed everyone present including the soldiers. It hit the walls and poured onto the floor.

When His persecutors beat Him with their fists, more Blood poured out. It didn't just trickle, it flooded from His body.

Think of it! The Blood of Jesus Christ, the Life of God, poured out for you, on your behalf!

When the soldiers pressed the crown of thorns into His head, torrents of scarlet blood ran down His face. The Blood literally gushed from His innocent head. It matted His hair. It ran into His eyes. It streamed from His cheeks onto His chest.

The prophet Isaiah saw this by the Spirit years before the crucifixion and said, *"His visage was so marred more than any man"*

(Isaiah 52:14). In other words, Jesus was so torn and bloody, His countenance was unrecognizable. He hardly looked human! Once He was put on the cross, with massive iron spikes driven through His hands and feet, the fountain of His Blood continued to flow.

A Roman soldier speared Him in the side and the fountain emptied. *"But one of the soldiers with a spear pierced his side, and forthwith came there out blood and water"* (John 19:34).

Every drop of His Blood and all of His water poured out on the cross and into the ground for you. Once and for all, every drop of His Blood was poured out. The price was paid in full!

Matthew 27:25 says they called for Jesus to be crucified and said, "His Blood be on us and on our children!" But Jesus saw their hearts and knew exactly what to pray for them: *"Father, forgive them; for they know not what they do"* (Luke 23:34). Those powerful words of forgiveness provide cleansing, healing, prosperity, and deliverance from the power of the devil for us today! He knew forgiveness was the answer for them as well as for us to grant us freedom from the hand of the devil.

Let's all say, "Lord we accept and receive your forgivness right now!"

Isaiah 53:5 says Jesus was beaten, smitten, and *"bruised for our iniquities."* That means the generational curses of sin that have plagued you and all mankind have been utterly broken by the shedding of His Blood. The abuse you have suffered and even the mistakes you have made can no longer imprison you.

**They are no match for that
precious, powerful Blood.**

The Blood is greater than drug addiction and more powerful than sexual perversion. The Blood is greater than the effects of rape and greater than rebellion, lies, murder, sickness, disease, and the list goes on. All the pain and sin-enforced patterns of the past lose their power when you thoroughly understand and accept what Jesus did for you.

The price has been paid in full. None of us in our right mind would try to pay for something twice—especially when it cost so much. This is the reason we must remember just how much it cost Jesus to purchase our redemption.

It cost Him every drop of His Life's Blood.

He poured out His Blood for every one of us. We didn't earn or deserve it. We can't do anything now to add to the price He paid. All we can do is receive by faith the benefits His Blood has provided and thank Him for what He did.

On the day of His crucifixion, the Blood of Jesus began speaking and proclaiming. It'll continue to speak and proclaim forever.

Listen to what it said as it flowed out of His body like a well of living love for you and all humanity:

Father, forgive them.

They just don't know…

Mercy, Mercy, Mercy.

Mercy instead of vengeance.

Life instead of death.

Blessing instead of cursing.

See the Blood. *Hear* what the Blood is saying *to* you and *for* you. It speaks words of life. The Blood is preaching your freedom!

Prayer and Confession

*Father, I realize Jesus was crucified for **me**. He was beaten for **me**. He was whipped for **me**. He was pierced with the crown of thorns for **me**. His hands, feet, and side were pierced for **me**. I believe I am free. Jesus paid it all for me, the whole price. There's nothing left for me to do but accept that free gift and be grateful. I am forgiven. I am cleansed. I am justified, innocent, with no case pending against me. His Blood has made me holy in Your sight.*

Proclaim and Decree

I proclaim all the benefits the power of Jesus' Blood has given me and for my family and loved ones. I speak the Blood. His Blood is speaking for me in Jesus' Name.

Other Scriptures to Study

Mark 14:22-25

Mark 15:1-26

Luke 22:14-20

Day 6

Redeemed to Reign

*But God demonstrates His own love toward us, in that
while we were still sinners, Christ died for us. Much more
then, having now been justified by His blood, we shall be
saved from wrath through Him. …For if by the one man's
offense death reigned through the one, much more those who
receive abundance of grace and of the gift of righteousness
will reign in life through the One, Jesus Christ.*

—Romans 5:8-9, 17 NKJV

TO understand what the Blood of Jesus is saying to you
and about you, we'll have to look back at God's original plan for man. God's plan was much more than just
Adam taking care of the Garden of Eden. He was more than just
a "gardener."

Let's look at the big plan.

In the beginning, God created mankind to be royalty on earth.
He crowned the first man and woman with dominion and gave
them the authority to rule and reign as His representatives.
According to Psalm 8:5, God made them just "a little lower than

Elohiym," which can be understood to mean "a little lower than God Himself" and crowned them with "glory and honor."

In Hebrew, the word *glory* can mean weighty, splendor, and copiousness. The root gives us understanding that it can be heavy in a good sense, numerous, and rich. The word can also be translated to mean glorify, abounding with glorious things, honor, prevail, promote, and to be rich. *Splendor* gives us the understanding of great brightness or luster, brilliancy, magnificence. *Copiousness* can mean yielding something abundantly, plentiful in number, full in thought, present in large quantity. The Hebrew word *honor* can mean magnificence, ornament or splendor, beauty, comeliness, glory, majesty, excellency.

All these words put together describe God.

The Bible is telling us this. When God crowned the first man and woman with glory and honor, He crowned them with Himself! He clothed them from the inside out with all of His abundance, glory, richness, magnificence, great brightness, and splendor.

> *God is light and in Him is no darkness at all.*
> —1 John 1:5 NKJV

Adam and Eve were covered with the light of God. Talk about superstars! Not even a shadow of darkness dimmed their radiance. They reigned as kings in life. They occupied the highest position God could bestow and had power to prevail.

What a life they had! Untouched by evil, they enjoyed the perfection of God's creation. They lived in a place free of destruction, sickness, disease, failure, discouragement, depression, and sin. A place God had created and declared to be *"very good"* (Genesis 1:31).

Sadly, however, Adam and Eve's reign didn't last long. They soon fell from their lofty position. Sin entered the planet through their disobedience, and the glory and honor of God departed from them.

Suddenly naked and controlled by the power of darkness, they found themselves covered in shame. Adam blamed Eve and strife made its appearance. Fear and faultfinding contaminated the human condition. Adam and Eve bore children, and because seed produces after its own kind, they brought forth a fallen, sin-enslaved race.

From a human perspective, the situation was hopeless. The crown of royalty and life had been lost. God and man had been separated. What could ever bring them back to God?

Thank God, as believers, we know the answer—the Blood of Jesus!

His Blood—which was the very Blood of God—accomplished what no man could ever do. It blotted out the sin that through one man, Adam, had ruined the whole human race. It reversed the fall and restored us to our original place with God. As Romans 5:19 says,

> *By one man's disobedience many were made sinners, so by the obedience of one shall many be made righteous.*

Adam's sin brought darkness and death. But Jesus, by pouring out His Blood, brought light and life. He brought us God's Grace and righteousness, *as a gift in abundance!*

Therefore, the Blood is saying to us we can now:

> ...*reign as kings in life through the one Man Jesus Christ (the Messiah, the Anointed One).*
>
> —Romans 5:17 AMPC

Let this truth saturate your heart: Your right standing with the Father is not based on your works or your right doing.

It's based on the ransom paid by your Redeemer. If you've been born again, you have been bought back by His Blood from the slave market of sin. You now belong to God. He is your very own Father. You are His very own child. He has crowned you with glory and honor.

Remember, *glory* can mean weighty in a good sense. It means you are heavy with God's own abundance, rich in every way, and abounding with glorious things present in large quantity. You are excellent and adorned with magnificence.

Because of Jesus' Blood, there is no darkness in you anymore. You can now fulfill Isaiah's prophecy:

> *Arise, shine; for your light has come! And the glory of the Lord is risen upon you.*
>
> —Isaiah 60:1 NKJV

You have been translated into the Kingdom of Light. You are seated in heavenly places in Christ, the Anointed One (Ephesians 2:6). You occupy a high place and you *can* prevail.

The Blood of Jesus is speaking all these things to you. Believe what it says.

Give attention to the Voice of His Blood and transcend all limitations into that secret place of the Most High God.

See yourself as royalty, reigning over the affairs of life. You've got what it takes. Embrace the destiny God has for you.

> For "In him we live and move and have our being...For we are indeed his offspring."
>
> —Acts 17:28 RSV

Prayer and Confession

My Father, my Heavenly Father, thank You for giving back to me honor and glory and for restoring me to my rightful position in this life. I hear the Blood saying to me that I have been translated into a high place where I can rule and reign. I am seated with Jesus in heavenly places far above the devil. This Blood is for me! God, You are for me. Greater is He that is in me than he that is in the world. My Father is greater than all.

Proclaim and Decree

I speak the Blood of Jesus for myself, my family, and those who need to hear how free they are in Christ. I'm letting Your Blood proclaim deliverance and freedom in Jesus' Name.

Other Scriptures to Study

Isaiah 43:1-7

John 3:16

1 Corinthians 1:30-31

Day 7

You Are Forgiven

Blessed be the God and Father of our Lord Jesus Christ,
who has blessed us with every spiritual blessing in the
heavenly places in Christ, just as He chose us in Him
before the foundation of the world, that we should be holy
and without blame before Him in love, having predestined
us to adoption as sons by Jesus Christ to Himself,
according to the good pleasure of His will, to the praise
of the glory of His grace, by which He made us accepted
in the Beloved. In Him we have redemption through His
blood, the forgiveness of sins, according to the riches of
His grace.

—Ephesians 1:3-7 NKJV

SOME of the current-day church have neglected to give the power of the Blood its proper emphasis. As a result, multitudes of spiritually anemic, guilt-ridden Christians struggle from one Sunday service to the next plagued by fear and failure. There are those who don't really realize their Heavenly Father has provided supernatural ability for them to overcome in all the affairs of life. And they can't access that ability because it comes through faith in the power of Jesus' Blood! Their lack of knowledge about that Blood prevents them from believing and receiving all its mighty benefits. This has been true in my life and other people I know.

The Bible says,

> *Faith cometh by hearing, and hearing by the word of God.*
>
> —Romans 10:17

Therefore, faith in the Blood comes from hearing the Word about the Blood. It comes from hearing the Word the Blood is proclaiming.

What is the Blood saying to you as a believer today? We've been looking at some of those things. Let's see more.

Perhaps its most vital message is this:

You are forgiven and accepted in the Beloved.

Through the shed Blood of Jesus, you have forgiveness of sins, and there is nothing the devil can do about it.

Sometimes we toss around the words *sin* and *forgiveness* so casually we lose sight of what they really mean. The word *sin* refers to a crime with its resulting penalty. It can mean a fault, a grievous sin, and the guilt and punishment associated with that sin. *Forgiveness* can mean real freedom, pardon, deliverance, forgiveness, liberty, release from bondage or imprisonment, and a letting go as if the offense had never been committed.

This is the reason you can rejoice today!

Through the Blood of Jesus, you have been freed from the faults, guilt, and sin-induced failures that once held you in bondage. You have been delivered from the fear of eternal punishment. You no longer need to live a life filled with struggle, turmoil, and dread.

You can now enter into the rest the Blood has provided for you!

The Bible compares that rest to the rest God enjoyed on the seventh day of creation. On that day, the earth, man's home, was finished. God had provided mankind with everything they needed to live an abundant, victorious, and blessed life. With His work completed, God entered His rest.

Of course, He knew that Adam would soon fall into sin and mess things up. He had already set the plan of redemption in place. In the Father's heart, Jesus was the Lamb slain before the foundation of the world (Revelation 13:8).

Isn't that amazing? God provided for your forgiveness even before He created mankind! He preplanned your provision before time began. That's why on the seventh day, He could rest (Genesis 2:2).

Now, you too can enter that rest.

By faith you can step into all God has provided for you through the death, burial, resurrection, and ascension of Jesus. Through His Blood, you can enter into the rest of right-standing with God, knowing you are made complete in Jesus, and He has blessed you with every spiritual blessing in heavenly places (Ephesians 1:3).

When you know you are forgiven, there is rest for your soul. No more struggling in your own flesh is required. Forgiveness has come to you according to the riches of His Grace!

Isaiah 1:18 says it this way:

> *Though your sins be as scarlet, they shall be as white as snow; though they be red like crimson, they shall be as wool.*

That means no matter how soiled, there's no struggle for cleansing. All you need to do is receive it by faith.

You know what it's like to be fresh and clean from a hot shower? It's wonderful, isn't it? That's how you can live spiritually every day!

When Jesus said, "It is finished" on the cross, He provided a cleansing for you on the inside. He knew you couldn't wash that part of yourself. You needed help. Like a loving mother washes her newborn, He continually performs this cleansing for you. As you apply His Blood by faith to your life, He makes it possible for you to live free from all sin and unrighteousness.

Forgiveness is a Covenant promise that has been ratified or approved in and by the Blood. It is settled. It is finished. Agree with what has been done.

Because of the Blood, you can now say:

- I am washed clean.
- I am forgiven. I am not guilty!
- I have been given liberty and freedom.

John 8:36 says,

> *If the Son therefore shall make you free, ye shall be free indeed.*

Today, right now, Jesus' Blood is proclaiming this Word over you: You are free and forgiven. Your sins have been washed away!

Prayer and Confession

Lord, I come to You based on Your Grace, not my works. I approach You and enter into Your rest by applying the Blood of Jesus to my sins. I let that Blood wash me on the inside. I let it set me free from bondage and imprisonment. Right now, at this moment, it is just as if I had never committed those sins. It's all by Your Grace. I have faith in Your Grace to do for me what I can't do for myself.

Thank You, wonderful Father. I can relax now. I'm free. The Blood says so and I agree. The chains of yesterday are destroyed and washed away. I have come to a new place in You. Jesus said, "It is finished," and so do I. I'm starting brand new right now. Today brings new hope and life. It's a day of new beginnings. Thank You, Jesus.

Proclaim and Decree

By faith, I decree, "It is finished," and I enter into the rest of right-standing with God.

Other Scriptures to Study

Exodus 33:14

Isaiah 11:2-4

Matthew 11:28

Hebrews 4:9-12

Day 8

Out of Slavery and into Freedom

He has delivered us from the power of darkness and conveyed us into the kingdom of the Son of His love.

—Colossians 1:13 NKJV

THREE major things happened when Adam and Eve disobeyed God in the Garden of Eden. First, sin was introduced and became the rebellious birthing place of selfishness, shame, and separation. Second, sin perverted God's blessing and brought forth the curse which resulted in poverty, sickness, and death.

Finally, when Adam and Eve rejected God, they changed lords. They bowed their knee to the slave-king satan and came under his dominion.

They were transferred out of God's Kingdom of Light and into the devil's power of darkness, where they became slaves living in bondage to the laws of sin and death.

It was a great tragedy. Yet people have been repeating it ever since. As the Bible says,

All have sinned and fall short of the glory of God.

—Romans 3:23 NKJV

As a result, the curse is ongoing to this very day. Multitudes of people are in bondage to it with sin, sickness, death, and poverty abounding without even knowing why. Multiplied millions are living as slaves of the devil. They don't know there is any way out.

But—thank God—if you've put your faith in Jesus as Lord and Savior, your story is different! Through His Blood, you've been *"justified freely by his grace"* (Romans 3:24 NKJV). In God's eyes, it's just as if you never had sinned. You have been *"redeemed from the curse of the law"* (Galatians 3:13).

What does it mean to be redeemed from the curse of the law?

It means the fall experienced by Adam and Eve has been reversed in your life.

+ They fell into the devil's darkness—you've been translated into God's Kingdom of Light.
+ They fell into death—you've been lifted into abundant life.
+ They lost God's blessings—you've had them restored.
+ They became slaves—you've been set free.

What's more, you don't have to earn your right-standing with God through legalistic obedience to a list of religious rules and regulations. That's what the Israelites in the Old Testament tried to do. They tried to live by the Mosaic Law contained in the first five books of the Bible. That Law was handed down from God to Moses on the mountain. Over time, people added to it and it became increasingly burdensome. No one—except Jesus—could live by it. It was impossible!

Actually, that's why God gave the Law in the first place. He wanted to show us that it's impossible for us to become righteous by our own works. The Law was designed to show us our desperate need of the Savior.

Now through our Savior, we've been redeemed not only from the curse that came on mankind through sin, but also from the *constant sense of failure* that comes from legalistic living!

Take a moment right now and let this become a reality to you:

You've been redeemed from the curse and transferred out of the power of darkness. You are literally in the Kingdom of righteousness, peace, and joy (Romans 14:17) and no longer governed by the law of sin and death. The law of the Spirit of life in Christ Jesus has made you free (Romans 8:2).

Don't misunderstand me. The devil hasn't gone away. He's still the author of slavery. He's still trying to enslave Christians today. When we participate in sin, we fall into his trap. But even if we do, we don't have to stay there.

The Blood of Jesus has provided a way out!

Satan has no authority or power to keep you ensnared. You are no longer his slave. You are *now* in a *new* kingdom with new and better principles. You've been placed in this new kingdom by the Blood. The moment you agree and proclaim what the Blood says about your deliverance, you are brought back immediately into the freedom of God.

You don't have to play by the devil's rules. A new day has dawned in your life.

God calls Himself the God of the beginning (Revelation 1:8; 11:17; 21:6; 22:13). He is not the God of yesterday or even the God of a second start. He simply begins. He just starts from a given point. You too can begin right now. You don't have to start over but just simply begin.

There is no past in God, only the present and the future. Your future looks bright. You don't have to keep repeating the same old patterns of yesterday again and again. You can begin now by applying and receiving on a consistent basis everything the Blood of Jesus has provided for you. Jesus said,

> *The thief cometh not, but for to steal, and to kill, and to destroy: I am come that they might have life, and that they might have it more abundantly.*

> —John 10:10

Through His Blood, Jesus has given you an abundance of life. Not just a little life, but an overflow, more than enough, more than what is needed, enough for you and others.

Your sin debt has been canceled because of the law of the Spirit and life that's in Christ Jesus. You don't owe the devil anything anymore. Live free!

Prayer and Confession

Lord, I'm living by the new law of life that is in Christ Jesus. That law gives me freedom. I am no longer a slave to the devil and sin. I begin right now. I'm living in the Kingdom of Righteousness. I'm right with You because of Your Blood. I'm living in the Kingdom of Peace. I'm resting in what Jesus did and I've stopped trying to save myself. I now surrender to Your love. I'm living in the Kingdom of Joy. I have enough strength to overcome in every area by the power of the Blood of the Lamb in Jesus' Name.

Proclaim and Decree

I am the righteousness of God in Christ Jesus my Lord.

Other Scriptures to Study

John 8:31-36

Romans 5:17-19; 8:2

Galatians 5:1

1 Peter 1:2

Day 9

A Brand-New Creature with a Brand-New Covenant

And you know that He was manifested to take away our sins, and in Him there is no sin. ...Whoever has been born of God does not sin, for His seed remains in him; and he cannot sin, because he has been born of God.

—1 John 3:5, 9 NKJV

...new creature: old things are passed away; behold, all things are become new.

—2 Corinthians 5:17

NEW is a wonderful word! It speaks of fresh possibilities and opportunities. It carries no tinge of regret about yesterday's mistakes and no sense of the past's limitations. *New* speaks of something in pristine condition, undamaged by previous use and abuse.

Today the Blood of Jesus is saying this about you: You've been made brand *new!*

By faith in Christ Jesus you've been born again. You are a *"new creature: old things are passed away; behold, all things are become new"* (2 Corinthians 5:17). On the outside you may look the same as always, but inside you have a new seed of greatness in you. That seed is Jesus. Because He is in you, you have hope and a glorious future ahead (Colossians 1:27).

**Positive change can come now.
Things are just beginning for you!
Through the Blood of Jesus, you
have a New Covenant with God.**

A covenant is an oath, a sworn promise, a contract, and a formal binding agreement. It can be defined as a written promise under seal between two or more parties for the performance of some action. The word translated *covenant* in the Bible can mean to cut flesh. It's the giving of oneself totally and completely to and for another for the express purpose of joining them together to become one.

"Could Almighty God really want to become one with me?" you might ask.

Yes! Jesus confirmed it. He said in John 17:21 that His will and prayer for us is to be one with Him and the Father.

That's been God's desire since time began. He made both the Old and New Covenants with the ultimate intent of joining Himself to mankind. Starting with Abraham, the Old Testament patriarch, God called a people unto Himself. When those people fell into bondage as slaves in Egypt, He raised up Moses to deliver them. In great power, majesty, and glory, He brought them forth and established a Covenant with them.

That Covenant—the Old Covenant—was a system of works based on obedience to the laws of Moses. Since God's people continually failed to keep those laws, Moses secured forgiveness for them and kept the Covenant in force. Acting as a high priest, he took the blood of sacrificed animals and sprinkled both the book that contained God's Word and all the people. He sprinkled the blood on both the tabernacle and all the vessels of the ministry (Hebrews 9:19-21).

Why are those things important to know? Because they foreshadowed the New Covenant we have today!

Just as God's Old Covenant people were delivered from the slavery of Egypt, we've been delivered from the bondage of sin and satan. God has brought us forth in majesty and glory and established a Covenant with us.

But there's one big difference: Ours is a better Covenant!

> [We have come] *to Jesus the Mediator of the new covenant, and to the blood of sprinkling that speaks better things…*
>
> —Hebrews 12:24 NKJV

It's based on God's Grace and the finished work of Jesus. Our Covenant isn't established on the actions of a mortal high priest sprinkling the blood of animals. It's established in the Blood of God's own Son! He died on the cross as the sacrifice for our sins.

He rose from the grave, ascended to heaven, and sprinkled His Blood upon the altar in the Heavenly Holy of Holies as God's High Priest on our behalf.

> **With His Blood, Jesus purchased our forgiveness for all time and forever secured our New Covenant. He joined us to the Father and made us one spirit with Him (1 Corinthians 6:17).**

What Moses did under the Old Covenant was just a foreshadowing of what is ours under the New—Moses sprinkled the book and the people. Today, the Word of God comes alive for us when the Blood of Jesus is applied. Moses sprinkled the tabernacle and the vessels. Today Jesus cleanses us with His Blood and we become temples of the Holy Ghost, vessels of honor, set apart and fit for the Master's use, prepared unto every good work (2 Timothy 2:21).

You, as a believer, are not just an "old sinner saved by grace" as some people say. You're a brand new, Blood-bought vessel of God. You are the dwelling place of the Holy Ghost. You have great value. You were bought with a price (1 Peter 1:19-20).

That price was the Blood of Jesus. You can now say:

+ The Father and I are one.
+ I have a New Covenant with Him that cannot be broken or changed because it's established in the perfect Blood of Jesus. I am forever forgiven and secure.

- Old things of the past are gone.
- I am a new creature, born again in the image of God.

Prayer and Confession

My precious Heavenly Father, I come to You now believing that You have planted within me the seed of greatness through the Blood of Jesus. I want that seed to live and multiply in me. You have made Covenant with me through Jesus, joining me to You in the very same way that You and Jesus are one.

*Thank You for giving me a new start, a new beginning. I begin right now. I can hear the Blood speaking to me—there's a new order of things starting for me this very moment. I'm moving from **the yesterday** into **the now** and looking forward with hope for what the future holds.*

I praise You and thank You, Jesus, for Your Blood. Because my New Covenant with God is based on Your finished work, I don't have to earn my relationship with You. I don't have to sweat it! I can just lean on You, speak Your Covenant promises, and expect them to come to pass!

Proclaim and Decree

I am brand new. I am one with Jesus and the Father.

Other Scriptures to Study

Luke 5:36; 22:20

Ephesians 4:24

John 1:14

Day 10

How Valuable Are You?

Knowing that you were not redeemed with corruptible things, like silver or gold, from your aimless conduct received by tradition from your fathers, but with the precious blood of Christ, as of a lamb without blemish and without spot. He indeed was foreordained before the foundation of the world, but was manifest in these last times for you.

—1 Peter 1:18-20 NKJV

THE value of anything is established by the price someone is willing to pay for it. Let me ask you today. How valuable are you? You can find out simply by looking at the price God paid for you.

The Bible says He redeemed you with the precious Blood of Jesus.

The word *redeemed* speaks of ransom. It refers to buying back or freeing from captivity by payment of a price. The word translated *precious* reveals what's valuable, most costly, honored, esteemed, beloved, or dear.

Only a fool pays more for something than it's worth, and God is no fool. He knows the value of Jesus' Blood. He treasures it and considers the expenditure of it most costly. He honors, esteems, and holds it dear. And He poured out that precious Blood to ransom you from the captivity of the power of darkness and set you free from the slavery of sin.

How valuable are you?

The Blood gives the answer. It says you have been bought back with the life of God's firstborn Son.

Notice, you've not simply been bought. You've been bought back!

That's an important distinction. It indicates that in the beginning, you, me, and every other human being belonged to Him. He is the One who gave life to us. We are all His offspring (Acts 17:26-27). Each one of us can trace our family tree back to Genesis where God said,

> Let us make people in our image, to be like ourselves. They will be masters over all life…So God created people in his own image; God patterned them after himself, male and female he created them.
>
> —Genesis 1:26-27, my paraphrase

It was a glorious beginning, but then an awful thing happened! We broke away from God's pattern. We became rebels, renegades, and rejected Him.

Of course, Adam and Eve were the first to go. They listened to the devil and disobeyed God in the Garden of Eden. They fell from their position of authority and their image was changed. They could have run to God and asked for His forgiveness when they realized what they'd done. But they didn't.

Instead they ran from Him and the power of darkness swallowed them.

Even before it happened, God knew what it would take to redeem not only Adam and Eve, but also all the rest of us as well. It would take blood:

> For it is the blood that maketh an atonement for the soul.
>
> —Leviticus 17:11

That's why after Adam and Eve fell, God made coats from the skins of animals to cover their shame (Genesis 3:17-21). Blood had to be shed to make those coats. Perhaps it was the blood of a lamb, to represent the Lamb *"slain from the foundation of the world"* (Revelation 13:8).

With that first sacrifice, the plan of redemption began to unfold.

God knew that ultimately it would take more than the blood of animals to end the estrangement between Him and man. It would take Divine Blood. Sinless Blood. The Blood of His Son, Jesus.

God knew this stark reality before He created us. Yet He created us anyway. He counted us to be that valuable.

Oh, the Blood of Jesus! The Father esteems it as a precious treasure—and so should we!

Without it, we would have just a religion. The religions of the world have many of the same elements Christianity has. They have a name. They have their doctrines and belief systems. They have finances. They have concepts about the afterlife.

Many religions even believe in and about Jesus, but they don't believe in the Divinity of Jesus' shed Blood as the only way of salvation. And that Blood makes all the difference.

Let me ask you again now: "How valuable are you?"

In the sight of God, our omniscient and wise Father, you are as precious as the Blood of Jesus.

God honors that Blood. He esteems it above measure and holds it dear. As you do the same, you'll experience a life of total deliverance—total freedom!

The price for your redemption has been paid *in full*.

Everything you need has already been purchased. Shake off the insecurities of the past and realize that nothing is impossible to you because God is on your side. He loves you so much He bought you back with the incomparable precious Blood of the Lamb (1 Peter 1:19).

Prayer and Confession

Father, thank You for loving me! Thank You for considering me valuable and purchasing my redemption with the precious Blood of Christ.

Help me receive all the benefits You have provided for me through that Blood. I believe I receive the riches of Your Grace today.

I am encouraged because I know for sure that You are on my side and nothing is impossible to You. As I believe and trust You, I know that nothing is impossible to me either. The Blood of Jesus is enough to redeem my family, bring us prosperity, and deliver us from every scheme of the enemy. I taste and see that You are good. You are good to me all the time!

Proclaim and Decree

I am precious and valuable. I have been redeemed with the precious Blood of Jesus.

Other Scriptures to Study

John 6:48-58

1 Corinthians 11:23-26

Hebrews 13:20-21

Day 11

You Have Fellowship
with Your Father

For it pleased the Father that in him should all fullness dwell; and, having made peace through the blood of his cross, by him to reconcile all things unto himself...

—Colossians 1:19-20

IMAGINE what it would be like to have the perfect father—a father who is infinitely strong, wise, loving, and kind. A father who smiles at you and hugs you tightly. One who makes you feel like you can ask him for anything and tell him anything because you have so much favor with him.

It's a delightful thought, isn't it?

Every one of us at some time in our lives has longed for that kind of relationship with our father. It's a natural desire, divinely woven into our hearts. It's a reflection of what God originally intended for every child to have. It's a picture of the father-child relationship God's way.

However, in real life not many have experienced that kind of relationship. Even those who have wonderful fathers often sense there's still something missing in their fellowship with them. We've all found ourselves at times yearning for more.

No doubt what we feel is something of what Adam felt after he sinned in the very beginning. He had known what it was like to be God's own son (Luke 3:38). He had known the perfect Father and enjoyed a perfect relationship with Him. He had experienced the fullness of his Father's favor. Through satan's temptation and Adam's sin, that perfect union and fellowship with his Father was broken.

At the time, satan thought the relationship between the Father and His son, Adam, was eternally destroyed. The devil thought he owned not only Adam, but also all God's children forever. Reveling in the part he had played in stealing from them the favor of God, satan believed that he would be their eternal master.

He assumed mankind forever would be separated from the presence of God.

Although you and I weren't around in the Garden of Eden like Adam, our union and fellowship with God was also interrupted by sin. And we—along with all humanity—deeply experienced the loss. We knew in our hearts that something was missing, something was broken, and God was no longer our Father. Unable to sense His love and His favor, we felt like spiritual orphans longing for home.

But thank God! We don't have to feel that way anymore.

God made the way for us to come back home and back to Him! He put the plan in motion even before the foundation of the world, knowing the father-child relationship between us would be broken. He also knew sin would so mar our concept of His Fatherhood that we wouldn't even be able to imagine it anymore. God did what only an infinitely powerful, wise, and loving Father could do—He poured into Jesus the fullness of Himself and His Life. Then He sent Him to live on the earth so that we could see what our Heavenly Father is like. "If you've seen Me," Jesus said, "you've seen the Father" (John 14:9).

Once God had demonstrated His Fatherly love for us through the life of His Son, Jesus, He sent Him to the cross to pour out the fullness of His Life for us.

Jesus reconciled us back to our Father by the Blood of His cross. Do you know what it means *to reconcile?* It reveals we can return to favor with that person, to restore communion between, to bring into agreement or harmony, make compatible, or settle a dispute.

Think of it. The Blood of Jesus, the blood of sprinkling that speaks on our behalf, has restored our broken relationship with God as Father. We are no longer separated. We can enjoy perfect fellowship with Him!

Today the Blood is saying to you, "You have favor with your Father. You are no longer an enemy. The perfect peace of the father-child relationship has been restored!"

Peace shows there's nothing missing and nothing broken.

Through Jesus, God has made you whole again. He has given you the relationship with Him for which you've been longing.

No earthly father can do for us what our Heavenly Father can, even though they may try with all their heart. His love for us is deeper, wider, and higher than we ever dreamed it could be, because He is love (1 John 4:8).

He loves you perfectly—no matter what! He can't help Himself. It's just the way He is.

Say it with me now, and then say it again and again!

God loves me. God loves me. God *loves me*. Yes, I believe my Heavenly Father God loves me. The Holy Father loves me.

Prayer and Confession

My Father God, I am so grateful You have reconciled me unto Yourself through the Blood of Jesus' cross. Thank You that I am no longer separated from You. I am no longer separated from love itself. Thank You, Father God, for restoring my fellowship with You. I believe You love me just like You love Jesus. Glory to You forevermore!

Jesus, thank You for revealing my Father to me. Thank You. Thank You. I can see my Father because I can see You in the Gospels through the eyes of faith. I know that You, Lord Jesus, are working together with the Father and Holy Spirit even now to show me how much I am loved.

Holy Spirit, thank You for opening my eyes to see such a depth of the love My Father has for me in Jesus' Name.

Proclaim and Decree

I am loved by my Heavenly Father. He has redeemed me from the hand of the devil. I have favor with God and man.

Other Scriptures to Study

Colossians 1:19-22

Psalm 5:12

1 Corinthians 1:9

2 Corinthians 5:18-19; 13:14

Day 12

Pursued by Perfect Love

For God so loved the world, that he gave his only begotten Son...

—John 3:16

According as he hath chosen us in him before the foundation of the world, that we should be holy and without blame before him in love.

—Ephesians 1:4

THIS is a simple but vital truth: God loved you so much that He gave. For God's love is simply *giving*. It is giving His best. Giving His all. Giving Himself. That's what He did when He sent Jesus to the earth. He gave us His love by giving us Himself.

What's more, He did it long before we ever gave anything to Him. He gave first! He chose us in Him before the earth was ever created. He planned to redeem us with the *"precious blood of Christ, as of a lamb without blemish and without spot...before the foundation of the world"* (1 Peter 1:19-20).

That means before the earth was ever created, Jesus had you on His heart and mind.

Before you were born, He loved you. Think about that. He loved you a long time ago. You can only love Him in return because He first loved you (1 John 4:19).

As believers, we've become confused about this over the years. Our religious thinking has run in the opposite direction from the reality presented in the Bible. We've developed the idea that God is playing hide-and-seek with us, and that He's always hiding from us and the burden is on us to find Him.

The reality is: God is and has always been in pursuit of us.

With an intensity that would rival the hero in any romance novel, He has been chasing us from the beginning. He has been running after us, desiring to give us what we need most—His love and acceptance.

Although there are rewards to seeking God and exercising diligence in His Word, we didn't start this chase. He did. He ran after us until we stopped long enough to accept Jesus as our life, love, and Savior.

Imprint this fact on your mind. God is the initiator in your relationship with Him. He is the original investor. He took the initial risk *and* invested *everything* into you. He laid down His life for you. He poured out His Blood for you.

The Bible says there is no greater love than this—that a man lay down his life for his friends (John 15:13).

Life and love are the same thing. Jesus' Blood and His life are the same as His love—and God gave them all for you before you cared anything about Him. He risked complete rejection. He gave Himself (love) to you first so that you could have something to return back to Him—genuine, selfless love.

What a love story! To be pursued by perfect love Himself!

More than 2,000 years ago, Jesus said He wanted you to experience the same love He had with the Father (John 17:26). He then went to the cross and poured out His Blood to make it possible. Now through that Blood, you have not only been accepted into God's family, but also your Heavenly Father loves you as much as He loves Jesus!

The implications of this are staggering. Once you grasp the reality that you are literally being pursued by God Himself—who loves you as only He can love—you will stop running! You will stop trying to chase God down! Determine to get a grip on this. Look again at that last declaration. Does it startle you? Do you wonder if God can really see you in such a positive light despite the sins of the past?

The answer is "yes," because He looks at you through the eyes of love. He looks at you through the Blood. As Colossians 1:21-22 says,

And you, that were sometime alienated and enemies in

your mind by wicked works, yet now hath he reconciled [you] in the body of his flesh through death, to present you holy and unblameable and unreproveable in his sight.

The words translated *unblameable* and *unreprovable* teach us we are unblemished, without fault or spot, morally without blemish, without accusation or reproach. They indicate that any charges leveled against us cannot be called into account. This is the kind of complete innocence we have in our Heavenly Father's sight. The Greek phrase translated *in His sight* can mean directly in front of, or presence of, as before the face or eyes of, before God.

Life is worth living when you know that your Father loves you and accepts you!

All fear melts away when you believe that, in His love, He sees you without spot, blemish, or fault, because He sees you through the Blood.

Prayer and Confession

Father God, I believe You love me. I know I can only love You because You first loved me. I believe You are out to make life better for me. Your love for me is bringing me to the place where all fear is gone. I can see Your plan clearly now. I proclaim the Blood of Jesus because His Blood made it possible for me to be loved by You, my precious Heavenly Father.

Jesus, You're wonderful. You reconciled me to Yourself even when I was alienated from You and acting like Your enemy. Your Blood presents me holy, without blame and without accusation in the sight of God, my Father. Thank You, Jesus, for Your Blood gives me entrance into that special place of love with my Heavenly Father.

Proclaim and Decree

I am loved by Father God so now I can love. I can love unconditionally just like my Heavenly Father.

Other Scriptures to Study

John 14:21-23; 17:26

1 John 3:11

Romans 5:8; 8:35-39

Ephesians 2:4-7

Titus 3:4-7

Day 13

A New Person with a New Purpose

Therefore if any man be in Christ, he is a new creature: old things are passed away; behold, all things are become new. And all things are of God, who hath reconciled us to himself by Jesus Christ, and hath given to us the ministry of reconciliation; to wit, that God was in Christ, reconciling the world unto himself, not imputing their trespasses unto them; and hath committed unto us the word of reconciliation. Now then we are ambassadors for Christ.... For he hath made him to be sin for us, who knew no sin; that we might be made the righteousness of God in him.

—2 Corinthians 5:17-21

THE Blood of Jesus says this about you today: "You are a new person with a new purpose. You have the ministry of reconciliation. You are an ambassador for Christ."

Being an ambassador of Christ means you are a diplomatic agent of the highest rank in God's Kingdom. You are accredited as His authorized representative. You are appointed to be His messenger to go tell the world, "God is not mad at you. He's done something about your sin. He has made you righteous through the Blood of Jesus Christ."

What gives you the right to deliver such an important message?

First of all, you are living proof that it's true!

God has done something for you that you couldn't have done for yourself. He has made you a brand-new creature in Christ Jesus. Your old, sin-dominated self is dead and gone—passed away! New life has begun for you.

That new life would have been impossible for you to attain through your own human efforts or works. It's yours only by God's Grace and through His Blood by faith. Therefore, because of the great work the Lord has done in you, you can boldly tell others from experience, "What God has done for me, He will do for you! You too can have a new life, paid for in full by the Blood."

That's good news! People need to hear it!

Many are confused about who God is and what His intentions toward them are. They have the idea He is keeping a score card or sin ledger so He can punish them for everything they've done wrong. They don't realize Jesus poured out His Blood to secure forgiveness for their sin and the only sin that can send them to hell is an adamant refusal to believe and accept what Jesus has done for them.

God wants the whole world to know this!

That's why He has appointed all of us, as believers, to be agents of His Gospel. It's why He has called us to communicate His goodness to this religiously brainwashed culture.

If you're ever tempted to feel you aren't qualified to fulfill that call, read what Jesus said just before He went to the cross. Knowing His time on earth was coming to an end, He explained how His ministry would continue:

> ...*as my Father hath sent me, even so send I you.*
>
> —John 20:21

That verse is still speaking to all of us today. We can do it!

This is the heart of God, the will of God, and the plan of God to you and for you. He made you a new person with a new purpose! He reconciled you to Himself and then promoted you to the position of His ambassador. God Himself has given you this rank.

> *Behold, the kingdom of God is within you.*
>
> —Luke 17:21

You have what the world desperately needs. The Blood is testifying to it even now, "You are a minister of reconciliation."

Prayer and Confession

Father God, it's such a joy to know that You aren't upset or angry with me or anyone else. Thank You for making me brand new, for making me a new person with a new purpose! I am grateful that You have given me a ministry, and that You have counted me worthy to speak and share for You. I'm encouraged to know You trust me with the priceless gift of sharing Jesus with the world. How wonderful it is that You allow me to tell others how much You love them. This could only be possible through the Blood of Jesus.

Jesus, once again, You've blessed me beyond measure. I am filled with joy, gladness, and thanksgiving for all You've accomplished in me and for me. I give You thanks. Help me through the power of the Holy Spirit to be a witness for You, to boldly proclaim Your love and life as a gift to all mankind in Jesus' Name.

Proclaim and Decree

I am a new person with a God-given new purpose. I have new direction in my life through the Blood of Jesus.

Other Scriptures to Study

Isaiah 52:7

Isaiah 45:24-25

Psalm 32:1-2

Mark 16:15-16

John 3:3, 5, 7, 16-18

Acts 13:38-39

Day 14

Free to Forgive

Giving thanks unto the Father, which hath made us meet to be partakers of the inheritance of the saints in light: who hath delivered us from the power of darkness, and hath translated us into the kingdom of his dear Son: in whom we have redemption through his blood, even the forgiveness of sins.

—Colossians 1:12-14

And forgive us our debts, as we forgive our debtors.

—Matthew 6:12

O F all the rich blessings that belong to us as Christians, one of the greatest is forgiveness. It's a powerful part of our inheritance in Christ Jesus. It's what delivers us from the dominion of darkness and sets us free in God's Kingdom of Light. Through the Blood of Jesus, God has made forgiveness available to everyone, for everything, all the time. As 1 John 2:2 says, *"He himself is the sacrifice that atones for our sins—and not only our sins but the sins of all the world"* (NLT).

Sometimes, however, we stop short of receiving all the forgiveness God has provided. We may be hindered by a failure to believe. According to Romans 10:9, forgiveness comes to us when we hear, believe, and confess the truth that we are forgiven. It becomes ours when we believe that. Because we've put our faith in the Name of the only begotten Son of God, we are not condemned anymore (John 3:17). If we don't believe that, God's forgiveness can't reach us.

Another thing that stops us from receiving forgiveness is not forgiving others. Jesus made that very clear. He said,

> When ye stand praying, forgive, if ye have ought against any: that your Father also which is in heaven may forgive you your trespasses. But if ye do not forgive, neither will your Father which is in heaven forgive your trespasses.
>
> —Mark 11:25-26

Trespass is like a slide or slip, a lapse or deviation, an unintentional error or a willful transgression. Many times, when others wrong us, it's just a slip on their part, an unintentional error. At other times it's a willful act of offense meant to bring harm to us.

In both cases, the Lord commands us to forgive.

Notice, He commands it. He doesn't suggest it. Why is He so adamant? It's for our good! He knows harboring unforgiveness brings forth bitterness and hatred (Hebrews 12:15). It hurts us and others.

"I know that's true," you might say, "but sometimes I just can't forgive people."

Yes, you can.

The Blood says so! It says, "You are forgiven, so now you can forgive." The New Testament epistles confirm it:

Be ye kind one to another, tenderhearted, forgiving one another, even as God for Christ's sake hath forgiven you.

—Ephesians 4:32

Forbearing one another, and forgiving one another, if any man have a quarrel against any: even as Christ forgave you, so also do ye.

—Colossians 3:13

This is an indisputable, spiritual reality. Once you've received God's forgiveness as a gift, you can, in turn, give that gift to others. Once you accept His forgiveness, you have the power to pass that forgiveness along. As a believer, you have the God-given ability to obey these instructions from the Bible. Forgiveness brings such freedom. It's amazing.

Any time you find yourself struggling to forgive someone, remind yourself of what Jesus has done for you. He poured His own Blood over all your sins and washed them away! As Colossians 2:13-15 says,

He canceled all record of the accusations against you. He blotted them out by nailing them to His cross.

Blotted can mean to smear out, wipe away, erase, or obliterate. Obliterate is to remove utterly from memory; to remove from existence; to destroy utterly all trace, indication, or significance of; and remove the tears, pain, event, and circumstances surrounding that event completely. The more you think about how God has blotted out and obliterated your sins, the more eager you will be to do the same for others. You'll want to forgive them to the point that all their sins or trespasses are completely removed from you forever.

Get a vision of that for yourself. See yourself forgiving others so fully that the sin they've committed against you never bothers you again. Trust God to remove their trespass from your heart so that you don't even see or remember it anymore. It's possible through the power of the Blood!

Prayer and Confession

My precious Father God, thank You for showing me the power of forgiveness that is mine through the Blood of Jesus. Lord, I believe I have the power to truly and from my heart, forgive those who have hurt me. I have the power to release and let go of all offenses, either real or perceived. I choose to forgive them and myself.

Right now, I ask You to search my heart by Your Holy Spirit to show me any areas of unforgiveness still lurking there. I ask You to utterly remove from my memory the wrong that has been done to me by (call out their name). As I forgive them, destroy all trace and significance of that trespass. I choose to forgive them right now.

Jesus, it's wonderful to have the power to forgive. Thank You for Your Blood!

Proclaim and Decree

I am forgiven. I am free to forgive. I make a godly decision to forgive others and myself.

Other Scriptures to Study

Matthew 6:12

Matthew 18:21-22

Luke 6:36-38

Luke 11:4

Luke 23:33-34

1 John 2:12

Day 15

You Can Forgive Others and Yourself

*Then his master, after he had called him, said to him,
"You wicked servant! I forgave you all that debt because
you begged me. Should you not also have had compassion
on your fellow servant, just as I had pity on you?" And his
master was angry, and delivered him to the torturers until
he should pay all that was due to him. So My heavenly
Father also will do to you if each of you, from his heart,
does not forgive his brother his trespasses.*

—Matthew 18:32-35 NKJV

ONCE we've received forgiveness through the power of Jesus' Blood, we are not only free to forgive others (as we saw yesterday), but also, we are obligated to do so. We can see why in the story Jesus told about the unforgiving servant.

At the beginning of the story, the servant was absolutely drowning in debt. He owed his king 10,000 talents of gold. That's a staggering amount. That price today in our terms could be into the trillions depending on the price of gold!

Could you repay trillions of dollars of debt? Probably not.

Neither could I. And neither could this servant. When the king required him to either pay his debt or be sold into slavery along with his wife and children, his only hope was to throw himself on the king's mercy.

> *The servant therefore fell down, and worshipped him, saying, Lord, have patience with me, and I will pay thee all. Then the lord of that servant was moved with compassion, and loosed him, and forgave him the debt.*
>
> —Matthew 18:26-27

You'd think the servant would have been so grateful that he'd want to go out and forgive somebody else's debt. Shockingly enough, he did just the opposite. He:

> *...went out and found one of his fellow servants who owed him a hundred denarii; and he laid hands on him and took him by the throat, saying, "Pay me what you owe!"*
>
> —Matthew 18:28 NKJV

A denarius equals maybe about one penny! That means this man's debt was only about a dollar! Yet the debt-free servant, instead of operating in the same compassion the king had shown him, demanded immediate payment.

> *And his fellowservant fell down at his feet, and besought him, saying, Have patience with me, and I will pay thee all. And he would not: but went and cast him into prison, till he should pay the debt.*
>
> —Matthew 18:29-30

When the king heard what happened, he was furious. He not only called in the unforgiving servant and rebuked him for behaving so wickedly, but also reinstated the trillions of dollars of debt! Then he delivered the servant *"to the tormentors, till he should pay all that was due unto him"* (Matthew 18:34).

The punishment inflicted on that servant shows us how seriously God looks at unforgiveness. He views our refusal to forgive others in the light of the enormity of what He's already forgiven us.

God has done far more for us than cancel trillions of dollars on a debt!

He's forgiven us of a sin debt so great that it would have imprisoned us in hell for eternity. He has utterly removed all our iniquities. He has completely removed them from existence and has destroyed all trace and significance of our sin.

Any sin debt owed to us by other people is nothing compared to the debt cancellation we've received from our Father.

Therefore, we are obligated to do for them what He has done for us. We must completely release and forgive others and ourselves.

We must allow the Blood of Jesus to wash all the effects of those trespasses away from us because we're so grateful we are forgiven.

If we'll do that, as we daily and deliberately choose to forgive, the Blood will cleanse us from the effects of the injustices committed against us.

On the other hand, if we choose not to forgive, we'll forfeit our own forgiveness.

We'll be delivered to the tormentors until we pay all that is due. And that's bad news, since we don't have any ability to pay for our sins! Forgiveness is the way out of this self-made prison.

This is the reason Jesus taught us to pray,

> *Forgive us our sins; for we also forgive every one that is indebted to us. And lead us not into temptation; but deliver us from evil.*
>
> —Luke 11:4

If we don't walk in forgiveness, God cannot forgive us. He wants to, but He can't. We wind up in bondage to the evil one.

Don't let that happen to you! Pour out your heart to the Father and ask Him to show you how to forgive with Christ-like compassion. Ask Him to reveal your weaknesses so that, through the power of the Blood, you can be made strong to forgive and forget. Ask Him to help you let go of hardhearted thinking and completely forgive.

He will do it! He knows you need His help.

He understands the pressure you sometimes feel when someone wrongs you and you're tempted to react out of emotion instead of responding according to God's Word.

In those times of pressure, the obligation to forgive creates a crisis of the will. It causes us to feel a little bit of what Jesus felt in the Garden of Gethsemane. There, He faced a crisis. It was greater than anything we will ever experience. Yet He triumphed over it by praying a prayer we must all learn to pray, "*Not my will, but thine, be done*" (Luke 22:42). Remember, He did it for us!

Through the victory Jesus won during His Gethsemane crisis, God has provided us with all we need to forgive anyone of anything. That crisis caused Jesus to sweat great drops of His Blood. Every drop of it cried out, "Mercy, mercy, and more mercy," as it fell to the ground.

The Blood is what gives you and me the ability to forgive. It has redeemed our will and separated it unto God. Through the Blood, we are empowered. We have authority. We've been given the right and responsibility to choose the higher ways of a higher kingdom.

The Blood is saying to you today, "You can do it! You can make the right choice! You can and must forgive!"

Go ahead and forgive right now—then continue to walk in forgiveness from this point in time forward. Right choices produce right results. Choosing forgiveness produces freedom. Even when that choice is difficult to make, it's worth the effort. Nothing compares to living free!

Prayer and Confession

*Father, I **believe** that Jesus shed His Blood to empower me to exercise my will to forgive. I am forgiven because I **choose** to forgive. I will not short-circuit my ability to receive forgiveness by refusing to forgive others. I choose right now to let go of every offense, no matter what others have done to me. I choose to live a life of perpetual forgiveness and eternal freedom in Christ Jesus.*

Thank You for showing me that forgiveness is an act of my will, and that my will has been redeemed by what Jesus did for me. In my heart today I can hear His great drops of Blood saying that I can and will overcome. I can hear it saying I have the power to forgive others, myself, and even You, Father, if I've had aught against You and didn't realize it.

I am rejoicing, Lord, because I can be totally free by letting go of unforgiveness and trusting You. As an act of my will, I forgive completely all who have trespassed against me. I realize now that I was hurting myself and others by holding on to anger and injured feelings. I'm free through the power of the Blood. I'm choosing today to allow His Blood to have control over my will from this point on in Jesus' Name.

Proclaim and Decree

I am free because I can forgive. I choose to let go of every offense.

Other Scriptures to Study

Matthew 6:12

Matthew 18:21-22

Luke 6:36-38

Luke 23:33-34

Colossians 1:14

1 John 2:12

Psalm 86:5

Day 16

You Are Sanctified from the World

Wherefore Jesus also, that he might sanctify the people with his own blood, suffered without the gate.

—Hebrews 13:12

AS a believer, you have an inward desire to live a life that's pleasing to God. You long to leave the sins of this world behind and be like Jesus. So, this will come as wonderful news to you that the Blood says, "You are sanctified from the world."

What exactly does it mean to be sanctified?

It reveals we've been made holy, purified, or consecrated; to be separated from profane things; to be dedicated unto God; to be purified, internally by a renewing of the soul, and to be cleansed externally.

Sadly, many Christians see such a life as practically unattainable, struggling to achieve it in their own human strength. Their motto is, "Try harder." No matter how hard they try, they feel like they're running in place, making very little progress.

Most of us can relate to that feeling. At one time or another we've all tried to work our way into sanctification. We've tried—and failed—to obtain by our own efforts what can only be received by faith in His Blood.

We can turn our failures into success if we will listen to what the Blood, the Word, and the Holy Spirit are saying.

According to 1 John 5:7-9, there are three who say the same thing. They all agree on this: in Christ Jesus, our sanctification is already complete (Hebrews 13:12 NLT). Then He was resurrected and sent the Spirit to make that holiness a reality in all of us who believe. Therefore, we are *"sanctified by the Holy Ghost"* (Romans 15:16).

This is so vital I must say it again. Jesus has cleansed you by His Blood and set you apart, once and for all, unto God. That means you don't have to work to "get sanctified." You are already "sanctified by faith" in Jesus (Acts 26:18).

When you accept this fact, your whole life will begin to change. Instead of sweating to obtain holiness, you can simply begin to cultivate the holiness Jesus has already given you. You can use your will to cooperate with the power of the Blood, the Word, and the Holy Spirit.

A truly consecrated lifestyle requires the work of all three of these divine agents.

The Holy Spirit begins His purifying work in you the moment you put your faith in the sanctifying power of the *Blood*. He continues that work as you renew your mind with *God's Word*. Jesus said in John 17:17 that we are sanctified by truth. God's Word is truth. As you allow this sanctification to be worked internally, it changes you externally. It sets you apart *from* profane things and *unto* God.

Both the *from* and the *unto* are important! If you focus only on being sanctified *from* sinful things like sex, drugs, and lying, you can slip into legalism. Your spiritual life can become a can't-do list. Can't-do lists tend to foster rebellion. They can open the door to religious deception by getting your attention on yourself instead of God.

Sanctification isn't just about things *you can't do!* It's not just about being delivered *from* sin. It's about being delivered *into* a whole new realm of living. Jesus came that we "might have life and have it more abundantly" (John 10:10).

Notice the words of the psalmist:

> *But know that the Lord hath set apart him that is godly*
> *for himself: the Lord will hear when I call unto him.*
>
> —Psalm 4:3

When you understand that the Holy Spirit, through the Blood of Jesus and the Word of God, has truly sanctified you unto God, your heart will change. Your thoughts will change. Even your words will change.

You'll begin to say things like this: Because I've been set apart unto God through the Blood of Jesus:

- I can do all things through Christ which strengthens me (Philippians 4:13).

- I can present my body as a living sacrifice, holy, acceptable unto God (Romans 12:1).

- I can be holy for He is holy (1 Peter 1:16).

- I can hear the voice of the Good Shepherd (John 10:27).

- I can walk in the Spirit and not fulfill the lust of the flesh (Galatians 5:16).

- I can speak the truth in love (Ephesians 4:15).

- I can obey the truth through the Spirit (1 Peter 1:22).

- I can forgive because I am forgiven (Ephesians 4:32).

- The love of God has been shed abroad in my heart by the Holy Spirit, therefore I can love (Romans 5:5).

The Blood of Jesus has made you holy. It is speaking *to* you, *for* you, and *on* your behalf, declaring, "You are sanctified from the world!"

Stop trying to be sanctified or holy in your own strength.

Accept the testimony of Jesus' Blood and His love for you. His Blood makes you clean and pure, inside and out. He has set you apart for Himself because He loves you.

You are His very own handiwork, His workmanship (Ephesians 2:10). Believe it, and your lifestyle and behavior will reflect it. Believe that you are sanctified by the Blood, renew your mind to the truth of the Word, and your speech and lifestyle will be transformed.

You will be a vessel of honor fit for the Master's service. Your life will be clean. You will be ready for the Lord to flow through you to help others and fulfill every good work (2 Timothy 2:21).

Prayer and Confession

Dear Heavenly Father, I am so grateful that You have sanctified me unto Yourself through the Blood of Jesus. Thank You, precious Jesus, for suffering on the cross for me. Thank You for pouring out Your own Blood to set me apart for God. You have made me pure from the inside out. I ask You for the grace to express with my life what You have done within my heart, in Jesus' Name.

Because of the shed Blood of my Savior, Jesus Christ, I am sanctified. I have been delivered from darkness and translated into the Kingdom of God. I have been set apart from the profane things of this age. I am dedicated to God. I hear the voice of the Good Shepherd. I do those things that the Spirit of God shows me to do. I cooperate with the Holy Spirit, the Word, and the Blood so that God can work this sanctification in me from the inside out. The Blood of Jesus speaks for me, "You are sanctified unto God," in Jesus' Name.

Proclaim and Decree

I am holy by the power of the Blood. I am sanctified and made whole by the Blood.

Other Scriptures to Study

John 17:19

Hebrews 10:14

Acts 20:32

Romans 15:16

1 Corinthians 1:2, 30

1 Corinthians 6:9-11

Day 17

Peace: God's Gift of Love to You

Therefore being justified by faith, we have peace with God through our Lord Jesus Christ.

—**Romans 5:1**

WEALTHY people usually write out a will before they die. They make a list of their earthly possessions and tell their heirs what they are to receive. In a sense, that's what Jesus did just hours before He went to the cross. He told His beloved disciples what they would receive from Him after He left the earth.

Knowing that rough times were ahead for them, this was among the last things He said, "*Peace I leave with you, my peace I give unto you*" (John 14:27).

It always amazes me to think about what else Jesus could have said at that moment. For instance, He could have talked exclusively about love. After all, everyone needs love, and plenty of it, and He is love. Right then, Jesus chose a different emphasis. He said, "You guys will have to walk in peace in order to make it. So, I'm giving you My peace."

Why did Jesus consider peace such a major issue?

Peace is the necessary ingredient that sustains us through every crisis. It makes the difference between success and failure in every area of our life. Without peace, human beings are miserable. When others are upset with us—especially those who hold positions of authority in our lives or our loved ones—we're a mess without peace.

That's the reason in your relationship with God, peace must be the starting point.

God created you for peace. He designed you to function in peace. For you to have perfect harmony with Him that produces peace, understand that He is not upset, angry, or mad at you. You have to know that the Blood of Jesus is saying, "You have peace with the Father!"

Jesus, having made peace through the Blood of His cross, has reconciled you to God (Colossians 1:20). You and your Father are on talking terms now. There is no strife or division between the two of you. Because you are justified by faith in Jesus' Blood, you've become an heir of the "Covenant of Peace" (Hebrews 13:20).

Once you realize that you and God are at peace, you begin to enjoy the good life!

Your soul is nourished and flourishes as you rejoice in His favor. Fear loses its grip, and you're comforted. You can have new boldness, confidence, and courage because you know that your Heavenly Father isn't upset with you! Everything Jesus has provided for you hinges on this peace. It is so central to your salvation experience that God wove peace in His very Name. As the prophet Isaiah said,

> *His name shall be called Wonderful, Counsellor, The mighty God, The everlasting Father, The Prince of Peace.*
> —Isaiah 9:6

Think of it—the everlasting Father and the Prince of Peace are the same! Your Father is peace personified. You and He can enjoy a wonderful relationship. Peace is His gift of love to you. All you have to do is receive it. Every time you allow the Blood of Jesus to speak to you and for you, peace will come.

Remember when the storms of life are raging and the waves are about to take your boat down, this is when you need to overcome the world's system and defeat the devil with peace. Agree with the Blood.

Proclaim *peace* in the Name of Jesus, and the "God of peace" shall bruise satan under your feet (Romans 16:20).

Prayer and Confession

*Heavenly Father, I am so glad to know that You are not angry with me. I'm so grateful that Jesus has made it possible for You and me to be in harmony. What a joy it is to be able to talk to You and have a good relationship with You! Thank You, Jesus, because of the power of Your Blood there is no strife between the Father and me. I allow Your Blood to speak **to** me, **for** me, and to stop the raging storms and make peace for me in the midst of any situation.*

*Jesus, because of Your Blood, I have a Covenant of Peace. I agree with what You did. Now I can hear your Blood speaking **peace, peace, peace** to me. I trust You with my life. I rejoice today knowing that You have overcome satan by Your Blood and bruised his head for me so that I can live in continual peace.*

Thank You, Father. Thank You, Jesus. Thank You, Holy Spirit, for giving me revelation of how I can continually live my life in Your peace in Jesus' Name.

Proclaim and Decree

I am full of peace continually because the "Prince of Peace" lives inside of me.

Other Scriptures to Study

Luke 2:14

Luke 7:50

Luke 8:48

Luke 24:36

John 16:33

Romans 1:7

Day 18

Say to the Storm, "Peace, Be Still"

For it pleased the Father that in him should all fulness dwell; and, having made peace through the blood of his cross, by him to reconcile all things unto himself; by him, I say, whether they be things in earth, or things in heaven. And you, that were sometime alienated and enemies in your mind by wicked works, yet now hath he reconciled in the body of his flesh through death, to present you holy and unblameable and unreproveable in his sight.

—**Colossians 1:19-22**

YOU'VE probably heard people say that Jesus brought peace to mankind. He actually did more than that. He *made* peace for us. *Made* can mean to create and cause something to exist.

Jesus is the maker of peace! He created it and delivered it to us through the Blood of His cross. It can only come from Him. As the Prince of Peace, Jesus has total and complete authority where peace is concerned—and His peace is wonderful! It brings the atmosphere of Heaven into our lives. When it invades our environment, it causes us to flourish.

When we don't have peace, we begin to deteriorate. All kinds of bad things start to show up in our lives. For example, disease is an indication that something in our body is not at peace or ease. That's why it's called *dis-ease*.

Loss of harmony with loved ones and friends or a lack of financial prosperity also can begin to plague us when peace is absent. We can find ourselves feeling broken, inside and out, as everything in our lives starts to fall apart.

"Can peace really be that important?" you might ask.

Yes! According to the Bible, the whole Kingdom of God operates through and by peace.

> *For the kingdom of God is not meat and drink; but righteousness, and peace, and joy in the Holy Ghost.*
> —Romans 14:17

Peace stabilizes our emotions in times of difficulty and uncertainty. It keeps us steady in our walk with God. If we're at peace, instead of letting go of our faith in the Word and in Jesus' Blood when we're under pressure, we can stand strong and let them work effectively in our lives.

These days the world is crying out for peace and trying to make peace treaties. But the greatest peace treaty of all time has already been established for you: the Covenant of Peace ratified by the Blood of Jesus Christ, the Maker of Peace.

When all is said and done, His peace is the only peace that will last forever.

Take a moment and allow that peace to settle, strengthen, and establish you. Listen to what the Blood is speaking *to* you and *for* you.

It's saying you will emerge from it as an overcomer by the power of God. So, agree with the following:

+ Everything is going to be okay. These troubles will pass.

+ These difficulties and trials are seasonal. The season is now ending.

+ No more worrying. No more fretting.

+ Peace is part of my inheritance. I don't have to strive or work for it.

+ Jesus has given peace to me as a gift of His redeeming love through the power of His Blood.

There was a time during Jesus' ministry when His disciples desperately needed to hear such words. A storm was threatening to sink their boat one dark night in the middle of the Sea of Galilee. They cried out, "Master, don't You care that we're about to perish?"

Jesus, who was sleeping in the back of the boat at the time, arose and rebuked the wind. He said to the sea,

> *Peace, be still. And the wind ceased, and there was a great calm.*
>
> —Mark 4:39

The devil himself sent that storm and got mad when Jesus stopped it. He went after Jesus and eventually nailed Him to the cross. He thought he'd silenced Him forever. He thought no one ever again would hear the Master say, "Peace, be still."

Satan couldn't shut Jesus' mouth and he never will!

When Jesus' Blood fell on the ground, it started speaking peace and still is speaking loudly today over the turbulence that threatens you.

Accept what the Blood is saying *to* you and *for* you. Rejoice over it. Believe it. Open your mouth and boldly affirm your faith in the Covenant of Peace. Say what Jesus said. Say what His Blood is saying. Speak to the turmoil that has risen up against you and say, "Peace, be still!"

Let Jesus be the Prince of Peace in you.

Prayer and Confession

Thank You, Father God. You knew exactly what You were doing when You created the plan of salvation. You knew His Blood would overcome the devil and all his works. I'm so thankful and grateful today for my Blood-bought Covenant of Peace. Thank You for teaching me how to live in that Covenant. Thank You for showing me how to walk in such peace that I am never rattled by any situation. Thank You that I will always know what to do and when to do it. All because I am in perfect peace!

Lord Jesus, I can lay down at night and sleep because of Your peace. I can increase in financial prosperity, overall health, and wellness because of Your peace. I can enjoy restored relationships with other believers because we are knit together in peace, bonded by love and unified by faith in Your Blood. I am whole, sound in my mind and body. Thank You for helping me to choose peace!

Proclaim and Decree

I choose to allow the peace of God to govern my life.

Other Scriptures to Study

Ephesians 4:3, 13

Galatians 5:22

1 Thessalonians 3:12,13

Colossians 3:15

Day 19

His Blood Says You're Innocent

For if the blood of bulls and of goats, and the ashes of an heifer sprinkling the unclean, sanctifieth to the purifying of the flesh: How much more shall the blood of Christ, who through the eternal Spirit offered himself without spot to God, purge your conscience from dead works to serve the living God?

—Hebrews 9:13-14

GUILTY! We all know what it's like to wear that label and to hear the accusations of our conscience and feel consumed by remorse and shame.

We've all done or said things we later regretted and spent days, months, or even years rehearsing what we should've, would've, or could've done.

As a believer, you probably know how it goes—you ask the Lord to forgive you and He does. But the guilt persists anyway. Condemnation is a well-fashioned, deadly weapon of the enemy hanging over you day and night. Reminding you again and again of the sin you committed. The devil paints a portrait for you to look at—a portrait of yourself that's so ugly that you're tempted to give up on your faith altogether and completely.

Getting rid of such guilt can be a huge problem.

The devil likes to torment people. Especially if you have a tender conscience, he'll work hard to overwhelm you with feelings of condemnation.

If you want to know why he's so persistent, just look in the Word. It says that a clear conscience is crucial to our faith. Without it, even the most committed Christians can end up shipwrecked (1 Timothy 1:19).

When our conscience is yelling at us, reminding us of our sins, faults, and failures, we feel unworthy to receive anything from God. Our confidence in our relationship with Him is weakened. We find it hard to believe He loves us and will keep His Word to us.

That's why the Bible tells us to hold on to our faith with a pure conscience (1 Timothy 3:9). A guilty conscience will hold us hostage! It will stop us from believing God!

What can you do when you find yourself in that condition? Listen to the Voice of Jesus' Blood.

His Blood speaks better things about you! It says good things even when the devil and your condemning conscience are saying bad things (Hebrews 12:22-25 NLT). The Blood of Jesus always declares "not guilty and innocent!"

Better yet, the power in that Blood can heal your wounded conscience and restore you to wholeness. It can wash you and purify you. It can give you a clean slate and make you totally innocent.

If you think that's too good to be true, think again.

No matter what you've done and no matter what you've experienced, absolute innocence is available to you as a child of God. It's yours through the Blood and God's redemptive plan. God first began to reveal that plan back in Old Testament times. He prescribed certain sacrifices that cleansed people of guilt—the guilt from wrongs they had committed.

He prescribed other sacrifices that removed the shame people feel—the shame resulting from things that had happened to them over which they had no control. For example, God made provisions in the Old Testament law for young ladies who had been raped. Through a blood sacrifice, He made a legal way for them to be pronounced clean from the shame and dishonor they'd suffered.

Those Old Covenant rituals were a type and shadow of the better things God provided for us through the New Covenant!

We are justified by the Blood of Jesus (Romans 5:9). We're not only cleansed from the sins we've committed, but we're cleansed from the *effects* of the sins that have been committed against us. We've literally been made innocent in every way.

There is a profound difference in being pronounced *not guilty* and actually being *made innocent!*

When you're made innocent, God does more for you than erase the tears and the pain caused by events in your past—He actually wipes out the events themselves. He removes them so thoroughly that, as far as you and He are concerned, they never happened.

This is what it means to be justified by the Blood! It means to be made just as if I'd never sinned—just as if I'd never been abused.

Do you realize what you can do if you grasp this reality?

You can allow the Blood of Jesus to heal wounds left in your soul by the past. Just as you might apply antibiotic cream to an infected area of your skin, you can verbally apply Jesus' Blood by faith to the memories of every guilt-invoking, shame-inducing event. You can watch those memories begin to fade until all their effects completely disappear.

Believe this today and get rid of the guilty label. Become as innocent as a child again!

Prayer and Confession

Father, I believe. I believe. I believe in the power of the Blood of Jesus to erase all those bad memories and heal me completely from the effects of the sins I've committed against myself or others, as well as those sins that were committed against me. All of them are washed away, blotted out forever because of Jesus' Blood. I receive this inside me right now and I change my thinking about the past.

I refuse to hear those accusations from the enemy anymore. I will not allow the devil to lie to me again. The truth is I'm free! Glory to God forevermore!

I praise and thank You, my Father, because of Your great love for me. Holy Spirit, you are amazing. Jesus, You are wonderful. Thank You.

Proclaim and Decree

I am innocent by the power of the Blood of Jesus.

Other Scriptures to Study

Deuteronomy 22:22-26

Revelation 1:5,6

Hebrews 10:22

Day 20

Overcoming the Accuser

The accuser of our brethren is cast down, which accused them before our God day and night. And they overcame him by the blood of the Lamb, and by the word of their testimony.

—**Revelation 12:10-11**

THERE'S a reason the devil is known in the Bible as "the accuser of the brethren." He's a merciless master at the art of attacking believers with an onslaught of blame.

If you've ever been the target of his accusations, you know how vile and virulent they can be. They often come in the night while you are trying to sleep. Haunting thoughts assault you, replaying like movies on the canvas of your mind. You feel helpless as you watch those same reruns over and over again—images of failed relationships, of wrong things you did, words you spoke, words spoken to you.

Even in daylight, plaguing thoughts of unspeakable things done to you cast shadows of shame and depression, shadows too dark and deep for words. You might be having a good day until something happens that triggers the memories. Then the devil pounces and points his finger at you, smothering you with blame all over again.

No question about it, such attacks can be intense. Even in the midst of them, there's good news—you are not facing them alone. There is hope. You can overcome the accuser by the Blood of the Lamb and the word of your testimony (Revelation 12:11).

The word of your testimony is your personal proclamation of the power that's in the Blood of Jesus. It's your declaration of the fact His Blood has set you free from anything and everything less than Heaven's best that has occurred in your life.

One day while praying, I heard the Lord ask something startling: "What does Revelation 12:11 say?"

"We overcome him by the Blood of the Lamb and the word of our testimony," I quickly replied.

Then He asked, "What does verse ten say?" I quickly read verse ten. There it was: *the accuser of the brethren.*

The Lord asked me another question. "Have you ever wondered why I referred to the enemy as the accuser of the brethren instead of the mass murderer, the hater of mankind, the author of fear, the child abuser, or the thief?" (The list went on and on.)

Suddenly, revelation dawned on me. I saw it!

The devil is called the accuser of the brethren in the final book of the Bible because the worst thing Christians will have to overcome is the accusations made against them by the devil himself!

Accusations have the power to literally take us down and stop us in our tracks.

Isn't that surprising? Who would have ever guessed that in the last days described in the Book of Revelation while the earth is being burned up, millions are dying amidst starvation, sickness, and calamity, the accuser with his accusations will be the greatest enemy Christians have to face?

This is important for us to know! We're moving into the last days right now!

That means we must be especially on guard against the accuser. We must be ever aware of his efforts to trap us in a never-ending cycle of condemning self-evaluation.

If we allow him to torment us about the past—about poor decisions we've made, mistakes, personal sins and betrayals we've suffered—he'll have us right where he wants us: under his accusing thumb.

That's not where we belong! The Bible says we've been seated with Christ Jesus in heavenly places, far above principalities and powers (Ephesians 2:6). We're supposed to keep him under our feet.

How can we do that? By the power of Jesus' Blood.

When you train yourself to answer the accuser and his accusations by telling him what God's Word says about the overcoming power in the Blood, he can't do anything but leave!

Let me say it again,

The power to overcome the accuser is in the Blood of Jesus and what we say and believe about the Blood.

Allow this revelation to go deep inside you. Swing it like a sword and cut yourself free from all the stupid, condemning thoughts the devil has tried to use to defeat you.

The Blood of the Lamb and the Word of God will work for you if you'll put it to work. So, start talking! Start testifying about the power of Jesus' Blood. Proclaim what the Blood says until the devil covers his ears and runs away in stark terror. Make the accuser sorry he ever messed with you.

Prayer and Confession

Our Father, how wonderful You are! You know what it takes to overcome the enemy of my soul. Thank You, Jesus, for Your Blood! Thank You, Holy Spirit, for revealing to me the power that's in the Blood! I am so grateful for the work You have done in my life.

I am an overcomer by the Blood of the Lamb and what I say about the power that's in the Blood of Jesus. I have overcome and will continue to overcome. Jesus has made me victorious through the power of His Blood.

Thank You, Lord, for always leading me in triumph. I praise and worship You for it. In Jesus' Name I pray, believe, and receive the victory now!

Proclaim and Decree

I am free from all the accusations of the enemy of my soul.

Other Scriptures to Study

Ephesians 4:11-16

Galatians 6:7-8

Day 21

Replace the Lie with the Truth

This is he that came by water and blood, even Jesus Christ; not by water only, but by water and blood. And it is the Spirit that beareth witness, because the Spirit is truth.

—1 John 5:6

Sanctify them through thy truth: thy word is truth.

—John 17:17

YESTERDAY, I talked about the accusations of the devil that are easy to discern—the mental movies he shows us of past mistakes and the condemning words he whispers in our ears.

Today, I want to address something that can be a little less obvious—the lies the accuser buries so deeply in your soul you hardly know they're there.

They can surface in the form of emotions. You're perfectly fine one minute and the next you're pouring out a bucket of tears, or erupting like a volcano of anger, or spiraling downward into depression. Although you pull yourself back together, you know it's only a matter of time until a tide of emotions will come out of nowhere and ambush you again without warning. You seem to have no control over it.

If that sounds familiar, this will help you break the vicious cycle. Begin to utilize those emotional outbreaks like you would a traffic light: red for stop, yellow for caution and green for go.

Each time those negative emotions rise to the top, treat them like a red light.

Stop and realize they're most likely an indication that you've swallowed one of the accuser's lies somewhere along life's journey. Deep down inside, you have believed something untrue and your emotions are responding to it. Maybe you've believed that you could never be forgiven or be able to get over that situation. When I say believing a lie that is untrue, I mean untrue based on what the Word says about it.

So, taking a cue from the yellow light, proceed with caution. Ask the Lord to show you what's going on inside. Ask Him, "Why do I feel this way, Heavenly Father? I'm cautious to the point of being fearful. What lie have I believed? Help me see the truth because the truth I know sets me totally free" (John 8:32).

The Holy Spirit lives inside you and He is always faithful to answer such prayers. He will reveal the deep-seated accusations the devil has brought against you that are producing those unpredictable emotional eruptions. The Holy Spirit will also direct you to truths in God's Word that will liberate you from the devil's lies (John 16:13).

Once you know the truth, you have a green light. You can go!

You can begin to change your thinking by believing that truth, confessing it, and applying Jesus' Blood over your emotions and your mind. Over time, the Word of God and the power of the Blood will wash those negative feelings and thought processes right out of your life. Eventually, they'll be blotted out so completely you won't even remember them anymore.

Through the consistent application of the Blood of Jesus, authentic freedom is within your reach. Jesus paid the price through the power of His Blood so you could be free (John 8:36).

"I want to believe that," you might say, "but the emotions I feel are really terrible!"

That's because the accuser, who is the original terrorist, is behind them. But don't worry, God is well able to deal with him. He's been defeating him for a long time. In fact, thousands of years ago, the prophet Isaiah identified the devil as "the terrible one" and said God stopped him in his tracks.

You don't have to be afraid of anything! You have the power of God on your side through the Blood of Jesus, the Word, and the Holy Spirit. What Isaiah said applies to you:

> The terrible one is brought to nothing, the scornful one is consumed, and all who watch for iniquity are cut off—who make a man an offender by a word, and lay a snare for him who reproves in the gate, and turn aside the just by empty words. Therefore thus says the Lord, who redeemed Abraham, concerning the house of Jacob: "Jacob shall not now be ashamed, nor shall his face now grow pale."

> —Isaiah 29:20-22 NKJV

Remember, the justification that comes through Jesus' Blood means your innocence is restored. His Blood erases the tears and the pain and even removes the time, place, and events that caused them—just as if they had never happened (Romans 3:25; Colossians 2:14).

That's the truth and it's far more powerful than any lie of the devil!

There's joy in believing the truth. There's pain in believing a lie (1 Peter 1:8). When you see a red light of uncontrolled emotions, then stop and listen to what the Word and the Blood are saying. Believe and receive their testimony. Let them reveal the devil's lie and replace it with God's truth.

You can do this! You can get the green light of God's great Grace. By applying the Blood and renewing your mind with the Word, you can go forward into a life of freedom, peace, and joy.

Prayer and Confession

Precious Holy Father, thank You. Thank You for sending Jesus for me so that I could be free. I believe and trust the power in the Blood of Jesus to cleanse me through and through. I believe the Blood of Jesus is making me whole inside and out. I believe those voices of rejection and accusation will no longer plague me. Father, I believe You are merciful and mighty to deliver me totally and completely once and for all.

I say now with confidence and faith, I am free from the accuser's voice. I am free. Whether the pain I felt was my fault or not, I'm still free. The Blood has done its job on me. It has cleansed my mind and cleansed my memory. Jesus, thank You for giving me Your life's Blood. Holy Spirit, thank You for giving me revelation that the voice of the accuser is now silenced. Thank You, Father. I pray in the Name of Jesus, my Lord and Savior!

Proclaim and Decree

I am free from the lies of the enemy. I receive emotional healing through the precious Blood of Jesus.

Other Scriptures to Study

Hebrews 9:3-28

Ephesians 2:18-22

1 Peter 3:18

Day 22

His Blood Says, "By God's Grace You Can Change"

I thank my God, making mention of thee always in my prayers, hearing of thy love and faith, which thou hast toward the Lord Jesus, and toward all saints; that the communication of thy faith may become effectual by the acknowledging of every good thing which is in you in Christ Jesus.

—Philemon 1:4-6

THERE'S one more thing you need to know about the accuser of the brethren. The lies he tells you and the blame he pours out on you aren't just meant to make you feel bad, they're meant to influence what you do. Ultimately the devil is out to control your actions, to keep you trapped in a life of sin, to push you into behaving in ways that will destroy you and everyone around you.

Here's how his operation works. First, he acts as the tempter to entangle you in sin. Next, taking his role as accuser, he condemns you for what you've done wrong. Finally, as the father of lies, he uses that condemnation to convince you that you're a bad person, a hopeless case, that there is something wrong with you that can never be made right.

Once you buy into those lies, they become part of your personal belief system. A belief system isn't made of passing thoughts and opinions. It's the bedrock of how you think. It's the foundation of beliefs that have been ingrained in you deeply throughout your lifetime.

The word *belief* could actually be translated *by-life* because people always live by how they believe. Their belief system dictates what they do.

I know from personal experience how much trouble wrong belief systems can cause. I also know what a hopeless task it can be to try to make them right. I tried to do it in my own life and failed miserably. Then one day the Lord showed me something that made a tremendous difference.

"How long would it take to change the course and depth of the Grand Canyon?" He asked.

Of course, I had no clue.

As I fellowshipped with Him about it, He told me that changing what I believe deep inside of me is like changing the deep grooves of the Grand Canyon. With man, it is impossible, but *not* with God. He shared that's the power of His Grace.

With God all things are possible!

The Lord helped me see that His Grace is the key to creating permanent change. His Grace is what saves us! It doesn't just save us from the penalty of sin so that we can go to Heaven in the sweet by-and-by, but it saves us from all the works of the devil in the earthly here-and-now.

God's Grace provides salvation for anything in us that needs saving or changing.

Some people have the idea that Grace just serves as a covering for sin. So, they keep on sinning and hope God's Grace will protect them from the consequences. Although God does offer us mercy when we repent of our sin, Grace isn't the same thing as mercy.

God's power is released in His Grace.

Far from being a license to sin, *Grace is the power to change!* It provides us with God's supernatural ability to overcome wrong thinking and wrong doing.

The day I received this revelation, it dawned on me that I could only experience genuine and lasting change by depending on God's Grace. With that discovery, I started changing immediately.

The same thing can happen to you.

How can you be sure?

As a believer, you already have faith in the Blood of Jesus. And through that Blood, you have access to God's very life. Leviticus 17:11 says, "The life is in the blood." Grace is a manifestation of Divine Life. So, all you have to do is call out by faith in Jesus' Blood and ask God for the Grace you need. He will give it to you in abundance! As you act on it and cooperate with the power of the Holy Spirit, you will change permanently. Your incorrect *by-life* system will be transformed (Romans 12).

Instead of believing and thinking about how you messed up and all the things that are wrong with you, you'll begin tuning into your true identity as God's new creation (Colossians 3:2). Gradually, you'll begin allowing the communication or outflow of your faith to become effective by acknowledging every good thing which is in you in Christ Jesus (Philemon 1:6).

When that happens, you'll stop rehearsing the lies of the devil and start singing out the praises of God. Instead of being overcome, you'll be an overcomer. Your joy will flow like a river, giving you strength to do what's right and live a life that's fully pleasing to the Lord (Colossians 1:10 AMPC).

Prayer and Confession

Lord, I believe I am changing. I believe I have the power of life on the inside of me standing strong. The power of Grace and the Blood together is making a permanent change in me. I will never have to fight those awful thoughts again because I'm bringing them into captivity. I'm letting the Blood of Jesus wash those thoughts away where I will never see them again as long as I live!

Jesus, I believe. Thank You for Your Grace which gives me the power to change. Thank You for the powerful Holy Spirit working these truths inside me to the point where I am established in my heart, in my belief system.

*I praise and glorify Your precious and powerful Name, the Name that is above every Name that is named—**Jesus!***

Proclaim and Decree

I am permanently changed by the Grace of God.

Other Scriptures to Study

Romans 14:17

Matthew 17:5

John 3:35-36

Ephesians 1:6-7

1 John 4:4

Day 23

You Are Protected

And he [Jesus] said unto them...Behold, I give unto you power to tread on serpents and scorpions, and over all the power of the enemy: and nothing shall by any means hurt you.

—Luke 10:18-19

BECAUSE of the Blood of Jesus, protection is available. If you will activate it, nothing can harm you. Nothing can by any means hurt you (Luke 10:19).

You can live in perfect security because by faith in Jesus, you have been delivered out of the dominion of darkness and into the Kingdom of God's dear Son (Colossians 1:13). He has *all* authority in Heaven and in earth. He has given you *all* power over the enemy (Matthew 28:18). Therefore, you can exercise authority over the devil and *all* Heaven will back you up.

Think of it! You have within your spiritual arsenal everything you need to paralyze the devil so his darkness can't touch you. You can so fully overcome by the power of Jesus' Blood and the words you say about His Blood, even satan himself can't get to you (Revelation 12:11).

You have nothing to fear because you are the one with the authority and power in the Name of Jesus!

Freedom begins when you choose to believe this is true. Exercise your will and believe it today. Believe you aren't subject to the devil's darkness anymore and begin to see yourself living in the light.

What does it mean to live in the light?

Read Psalm 119:130 and you'll see. It says the entrance of God's Word gives light. God's Word is truth (John 17:17). Any time you see the word *light* in the Bible, you can substitute the word *truth*. Since knowing the truth is what makes you free, the more you meditate on the Word, the more light will come (John 8:32). You'll start to see and the freer you'll become.

Say it out loud right now!

I am living in truth. I am living in light. Therefore, I am free.

Another word that can be substituted for *light* is the word *love*. The Bible says he who loves abides in the light (1 John 2:10). It also says there is no fear in love, but perfect love casts out fear (1 John 4:18). The darkness of fear always surrenders when the love of God enters the room. When you open your mouth and begin to tell the truth about how much God loves you, fear leaves.

Now, consider this. Nothing in Heaven or earth speaks louder about God's love for you than the Blood of Jesus! When Jesus was on the cross paying the price for your freedom, He was beaten so badly He could hardly say anything. The time came when He couldn't talk at all. Even then, His Blood had a Voice and it spoke of His love for you.

It's still speaking today on your behalf to all your enemies. It's saying that God loves you, and that He has provided protection for you from every work of the devil. It says you have authority and power in Jesus' Name—all because of what He did *just for you.*

The devil is defeated when the Blood speaks!

Release its Voice with the words of your mouth. Resist the devil in faith and he will flee (1 Peter 5:9; James 4:7).

I know this from an experience many years ago. A demon manifested in front of me and tried to scare me. I started rebuking him. He just stood there undaunted. Then, I rebuked him in the Name of Jesus by the power of the Blood. Then I said, "The Blood, the Blood, the Blood." Once I started speaking the Blood of Jesus, he started backing up and left my presence very quickly. He ran away because he knew he was no match for the Blood and Jesus' Name!

When the devil comes against you, you can do the same thing I did.

You can activate the protection that's provided to you by the Blood! If you'll do that, no matter what kind of dangers you might face, you can live in safety just like the children of Israel did in the book of Exodus. On the night of the first Passover, they applied the blood of the lamb to the door posts of their homes and then went inside. That night when the death plague struck in Egypt, the plague was forced to pass over them because of the blood (Exodus 12:7-23).

If the blood of animals applied to door posts could provide such protection under the Old Covenant, imagine what the powerful Blood of Jesus applied to our lives by faith with the words of our lips can do today!

Under the Old Covenant, the Israelites were living on spiritual "credit." Under the New Covenant, our bill has been paid in full. Jesus has come. He paid the price for all sin and became our Passover Lamb. It's time to rejoice!

Prayer and Confession

Father, thank You for giving me the Name and the Blood of Jesus. I believe I am protected. I believe my family is protected because I am applying the Blood to every area of our lives.

Jesus, You are our Passover. You are taking care of us as we abide by faith in the power of your Blood and trust You for protection and deliverance. Thank You, when the enemy sees and hears the Blood speaking, he cannot enter and has to pass by. The Blood closes every door of access so the enemy can't enter in against me and my family.

Thank You, Jesus, for helping me to see this truth. I am no longer in darkness. I am living in the light because of what You have done in me and for me. I believe I receive revelation and insight.

Blessings, glory, and honor to You. Thank You, Holy Spirit, for opening my eyes to this truth, in Jesus' Name I pray.

Proclaim and Decree

I am protected by the Blood of the Lamb.

Other Scriptures to Study

Isaiah 43:1-7

Acts 17:26

Day 24

You Are Accepted

To the praise of the glory of his grace, wherein he hath made us accepted in the beloved.

—Ephesians 1:6

REJECTION is one of the hardest things any human being can experience. The devastation that comes with it can almost be unbearable.

The first people who discovered this were Adam and Eve. They felt the pain of rejection for the first time when they disobeyed God and separated themselves from His love. Assuming He had rejected them, they ran away from Him even though He was trying to help them.

He found them and asked what they'd done. Adam reacted like we often do when we feel rejected. He blamed others for his pain. He pointed his finger at Eve and God and said his disobedience was their fault. Although Eve laid the blame more accurately on the devil, she too experienced her own double portion of rejection, feeling suddenly unacceptable not only to God, but also to her husband as well.

It was all a horrible, painful mess!

Before it ever happened, God had made provision. He had foreseen Adam and Eve's sin and the sense of rejection it would bring. He had a plan to make things right. Before the human race was ever created, He appointed Jesus as the Lamb slain from before the foundation of the world so that through Him, we all could be made acceptable again (1 Peter 1:19-20).

Take a moment right now and let this fact register in your heart—God provided for Adam and Eve's restoration, as well as yours and mine, before we ever sinned. He arranged to accept us into His favor by and through the power of Jesus' Blood, long before we were ever born!

Do you realize what that means?

It means God *never* rejected you or me!

Instead, He sent Jesus to take our place and bear the rejection we deserved!

That's why Jesus fully understands *"the feeling of our infirmities"* (Hebrews 4:15). He knows what it's like to feel rejected! He was despised and rejected by everyone, including His own family (Isaiah 53:3). When He was crucified, He even felt rejected by God, and cried out, *"Why hast thou forsaken me?"* (Mark 15:34).

This is the good news of salvation! Jesus came to earth and became our substitute.

He took on Himself all the sin of mankind and the rejection that came with it. Today His Blood is saying, "You have been made acceptable to the Father. You are accepted in the beloved" (Ephesians 1:6).

Because of the Blood of Jesus, we don't have to suffer the pain of rejection anymore. Even though people may reject us at times, we don't have to receive the pain of that rejection. We don't have to allow it to put an arrow through our hearts or shatter our emotions because Jesus has paid the price for us.

Settle this within yourself forever— regardless of what anyone else says about it, Jesus has made you acceptable.

Through His sacrifice, He has provided for you special honor. He has placed a grace on you that gives you favor in His sight and with others!

- *You* are special.
- You are one of a kind.
- *You* are unique in the eyes of God.

Jesus said, "If you've seen Me, you've seen the Father" (John 14:9). He knew you needed a father/child relationship to believe, feel, and know that you are accepted. He shed His Blood to show you how completely your Father loves and accepts you.

You can overcome rejection and the pain of rejection from any source at any time by applying the Blood.

HIS BLOOD SPEAKS

It is more powerful than any kind of rejection. It testifies that you are no longer rejected. You are now a highly favored son or daughter of the Most High God.

Your Heavenly Father accepts you not because of what you have or have not done, but because of what Jesus did for you!

- You can hold your head up high.
- You are somebody because of what Jesus did just for you!
- He was rejected for you in your place, so you don't have to feel that pain.
- God loves you. He really loves you. Jesus loves the real you through and through!

Decide now to believe it. Declare now,

> *No more rejection! I believe in the power of the Blood of Jesus that He poured out on His cross especially for me. I'm accepted in the Beloved Lord Jesus.*

Prayer and Confession

> *My Heavenly Father, I worship and honor You in my life, Sir, because You love me. You have accepted me, not based on what I have done or not done, but because of what Jesus did for me. I don't have to work to earn Your acceptance. Jesus did it all for me.*
>
> *I stand against and refuse any and all rejection in whatever form it may come in from this day forward.*

150

Rejection is not mine because Jesus bore it in my place. I will not suffer the mental and emotional torment of rejection because the price for my freedom has been paid in full.

Thank You, Lord, for honoring me. Thank You for giving me Grace, favor, and honor everywhere I go and with everyone. It's all because of You and Your love. I am so thankful and grateful for all You have done for me. You've made me feel like a complete person, like a first-class citizen with value and worth. I thank You for the Blood that has washed and cleansed me from all the pain of rejection.

Jesus, when You were on the cross, You were thinking of me. You were doing this just for me so that I would understand and embrace the reality that I am truly acceptable in Your eyes.

Holy Spirit, thank You for opening my eyes to see this special truth about how much God loves me as an individual. Praise and glory to You, Father, in Jesus' Name.

Proclaim and Decree

I am accepted in the Beloved because of the Blood of Jesus.

.

Other Scriptures to Study

Genesis 19:19

Psalm 84:11

Luke 4:18

Day 25

From Victim to Victor

In the world you will have tribulation; but be of good cheer, I have overcome the world.

—John 16:33 NKJV

Now thanks be unto God, which always causeth us to triumph in Christ.

—2 Corinthians 2:14

ARE you living like a victim or a victor? The answer depends on your mindset because the Bible says, *"As he thinketh in his heart, so is he"* (Proverbs 23:7).

A victim mentality comes from having a downcast, sorrowful, and defeated perspective. A victorious mentality comes from thinking in line with the written Word of God.

If you believe God is for you, if you believe no one can prevail against you, victory will start manifesting in everything you do (Romans 8:31).

Don't misunderstand me. I'm not saying overcoming the battles of everyday life will always be easy. Sometimes the battles can be tough. Even when they are, we can still win them because Jesus has already given us the victory through His Word, His Name, and His Blood.

You see, when Jesus went to the cross, He didn't just win one battle against the devil. He won the whole war!

He paid the entire price for sin and fully defeated it so you could overcome every trial and temptation with honor. He overcame the world so that by faith in Him you could be an overcomer and live in peace and joy!

Jesus is Lord and your victory has been assured by His own precious Blood. Now He is resurrected and seated at the right Hand of God to make intercession for your success (Hebrews 7:25). He's the author and finisher of your faith. He's praying for you like He prayed for Peter so that your faith will not fail (Hebrews 12:2; Luke 22:32).

Talk about a sure thing! Jesus has done everything necessary to make you a winner. By the power of His Blood, He has overcome sin, sickness, poverty, and satan himself for you. He has provided real and complete victory for you in this life and in the life to come.

How do you take hold of that victory?

Put your faith in what He has accomplished and consider it done for you, personally. Start believing that you are a winner! You always win and never lose! Conversely, the devil never wins and always loses. Jesus causes you to triumph (2 Corinthians 2:14). Because the Blood of Jesus has overcome satan himself, literally nothing is impossible to you (Matthew 17:20).

This isn't just positive thinking. It's our reality as believers. Jesus never intended for us to be victims. We are His victorious, Blood-bought Church. We should not accept defeat in any area. Instead, we should speak words of faith and acknowledge every good thing that is in us in Christ Jesus (Philemon 1:6). We are to overcome by the Blood of the Lamb and the word of our testimony (Revelation 12:11)!

Your words are extremely important.

When you speak about the Blood, you allow its power to be activated on your behalf. Things around you start lining up according to God's will. Demons start running away. Trials begin to lose their power and come to an end.

Make it a habit to speak daily of what the Blood has done for you. Get a hold of yourself and do some talking—some good positive Word talking. Meditate on being an overcomer instead of seeing yourself being overcome. See yourself on top of the pile instead of under it. Use your redeemed imagination and pull down every unbelieving, defeat-driven thought that would try to keep you in the miry pit.

You can do it!

Even if you can't seem to do anything but say, "the Blood, the Blood, the Blood," the power in that Blood will lift you up until you are shouting the victory!

Why look down when you can look up? Why think about who's done what to you, how things haven't worked out, and how many times you've failed?

It doesn't matter what happened in the past, you are *not* a failure. You may need to add some other spiritual qualities to your faith, but you are not a failure.

Dare to believe that and then get busy growing into the winner God has created you to be in Christ.

> *Make every effort to respond to God's promises. Supplement your faith with a generous provision of moral excellence, and moral excellence with knowledge, and knowledge with self-control, and self-control with patient endurance, and patient endurance with godliness, and godliness with brotherly affection, and brotherly affection with love for everyone. The more you grow like this, the more productive and useful you will be in your knowledge of our Lord Jesus Christ.*
>
> —2 Peter 1:5-8 NLT

> *...for if you do this, you will never stumble or fall.*
>
> —2 Peter 1:10 AMPC

Set your heart on obeying those verses and you will always win. You will be *"fruitful in every good work"* (Colossians 1:10).

Your circumstances don't determine whether you win or lose. Your faith, your belief system, what you *really* believe determines your victory. So, take hold of God's Word, the Blood of Jesus, and His Name until you are completely saturated with an inner picture of yourself winning in life!

Prayer and Confession

Lord, I do believe You made me a winner and not a loser. I am changing on the inside by Your Grace. The power of the Blood of Jesus is washing away all the negative, failure-filled thoughts I've had and changing them to thoughts of success in You.

Father, You made me a winner just like You are. You always win and never lose. I've been made in Your image and Your likeness. I can win in the outside world because I've already won on the inside of me.

I'm no longer a victim. I am victorious in You. I am an overcomer in all things because I believe Your Word. I will not accept defeat. I will only accept victory in Jesus' Name.

Thank You, Holy Spirit, for helping me see just how victorious I am in Jesus. The power to come up and over the top is in me now. I praise Your Holy Name.

Father, You created me to win and I am winning now because of the power You've given me in Jesus. In Jesus' Name, I pray. Amen.

Proclaim and Decree

I am overcoming at all times and in every situation by the Blood of Jesus.

Other Scriptures to Study

Psalm 92:4

1 Corinthians 15:54-57

1 John 5:4

Day 26

The Great Exchange

He was wounded for our transgressions, he was bruised
for our iniquities: the chastisement of our peace was upon
him; and with his stripes we are healed.

—Isaiah 53:5

WHEN Jesus went to the cross for you, He not only paid the price to free you from the spiritual effects of sin, but He also dealt with its physical and emotional aspects as well. He took stripes on His back so your body could be healed and made whole. He wore a crown of thorns on His head so you could think clearly and be healed emotionally.

Because Jesus loves you completely— spirit, soul, and body—He did a complete work on the cross for you.

He exchanged His righteousness for your sin and His health for your sickness so you could be righteous and in health. Through the Blood of His cross, He annihilated and overcame all disease, torment, emotional trauma, and psychological dysfunction.

[He bore] *our sins in his own body on the tree, that we,*

being dead to sins, should live unto righteousness: by whose stripes [we] were healed.

—1 Peter 2:24

The Blood that flowed from Jesus' head and back the day He was crucified cried out for mankind's full restoration and for vengeance against satan, who is the ultimate source of every kind of disease. It provided healing for every aspect of our being—physical, emotional, relational, financial, and social.

Sadly, however, many Christians today are still living dysfunctional, broken, weary, sick, or emotionally traumatized lives. Some are staggering under a back-breaking financial burden. Others are brokenhearted over the loss of a loved one and other heartbreaking situations. Multitudes are struggling to survive while the enemy uses the avenue of pouring lies into their souls to steal, kill, and destroy them.

What a tragedy! Jesus didn't come so we could merely survive! He came so that we could be victorious and enjoy abundant life (John 10:10).

He laid down His life so we could exchange *"beauty for ashes, the oil of joy for mourning, the garment of praise for the spirit of heaviness"* (Isaiah 61:3). He made *peace* for us through the Blood of His cross, and that peace has healing in it (Colossians 1:20). The opposite of *dis-ease*, His peace removes the *dis* and leaves the *ease!*

How can you receive that healing peace?

Consider Jesus! Think of the depth of the pain and agony He endured so that you could be made whole, healthy, and vibrantly alive.

Think of the sacrifice He made so you could have joy and gladness instead of mourning and sorrow.

Then, make a trade! Give the devil back his mourning and sorrow and take the joy of the Lord instead. Accept the oil of gladness and a merry heart which heals you like a medicine (Proverbs 17:22). Many times, when your emotions get healed, your physical healing follows. So be glad and shout because Jesus took upon Himself all your sicknesses and disease in every form and destroyed their power over you. Rejoice in what the Blood is saying *to* you and *for* you.

Appropriate that Blood on your behalf. The devil cannot defeat it. It's a weapon he cannot withstand. Arm yourself with it by believing in it, thinking about it, and saying, "By His stripes, I am made whole. I have a sound mind with healthy thoughts."

Spend time talking about the Blood. Pray about it. Write about it. Meditate on the Blood. Totally immerse yourself in the revelation of the power of the Blood.

If you receive a bad report from the doctor, refuse to let your heart be troubled and simply trust in God's mighty power (John 14:1). Rather than repeating the report that says you are not whole and healthy, believe and declare the report of the Lord. His report works (John 12:38)!

Whatever needs to be changed in your soul or in your body can be changed by God's Grace working through the power of Jesus' Blood.

If you will put your faith in God, that faith will work miracles for you and your family. It will move that mountain of negative circumstances right into the sea (Mark 11:22-23).

Healing is good. But being made whole is great. God wants you completely whole, inside and out. He created you to be a winner. He wants you to *"prosper in all things and be in health, just as your soul prospers"* (3 John 1:2 NKJV). So, proclaim the power of the Blood today. Say it over and over until it permeates every cell of your being and every part of your memory. Say it until you experience complete wholeness in every area of life!

Prayer and Confession

My Father, how wonderful You are. You've thought of everything. Through Your plan of redemption, you've done everything necessary for me to be complete in all things—spiritually, physically, and emotionally. Thank You for wanting me to be whole and for making provision for my wholeness, inside and out.

I'm so grateful that by Your stripes, Jesus, You've made the way for me to overcome the enemy's attacks against my soul and my physical body. I can hear Jesus' Blood crying out to me now, "Be made whole."

I believe. I believe. I believe that I am made whole. Be it done unto me according to Your Word. I am healed by faith now. My helper, the Holy Spirit, is enabling me to see myself enjoying a healthy life, filled with joy and peace. I can see my family and loved ones healed and living in abundance.

Thank You, wonderful Father, my dear Lord Jesus Christ, and precious Holy Spirit for empowering me to live as the winner You created me to be in Jesus' Name!

Proclaim and Decree

I am healed and made whole through the Blood of Jesus.

Other Scriptures to Study

Deuteronomy 25:3

Matthew 4:23; 9:35; 10:1

Day 27

You Are Washed and Clean

If we confess our sins, he is faithful and just to forgive us our sins, and to cleanse us from all unrighteousness.

—1 John 1:9

IF you've been a believer for very long, most likely you've already discovered this fact—even though you're a Christian, you're not perfect. From time to time, we all commit sins.

Thank God, you don't have to despair over them. As the verse above confirms, there is help! The power in the Blood of Jesus can make you clean again. It can remove every trace of sin. Grace is always available by the power of the Blood to help overcome any and all sins.

Because of the Blood, even when you miss it, you can act on 1 John 1:9 and say, "All my sins are washed away!"

Notice the word *sins* there is plural. That's important. It reveals that this particular kind of cleansing is yours specifically, because you are a believer. Before salvation, individual sins weren't the problem. The problem was sin (singular) or, in other words, the old sin nature. Because you and I had sin in our spirits, we were dominated by it. We sinned because we were sinners! We couldn't help ourselves!

You would still be in that situation today if it wasn't for this:

God did something very personal to solve your dilemma.

Because you are the object of His affection, He sent His own Son and not an angel or some other celestial being but His very own Son to take your sin, the sin nature, and the sin of all mankind upon Himself. He sent Jesus to be the sacrificial Lamb and take away your old sin nature.

When you put your faith in Jesus, you were transferred out of Adam's family of sinners into God's family of righteousness. You were born again. Your sin nature was changed. You became a new creation in Christ Jesus (2 Corinthians 5:17). Your spirit was set free from the sin nature (singular).

Your mind and body, on the other hand, though they've been purchased by God were not instantly changed. They've not yet been made new in the way your spirit has. They can be transformed more and more into the image of Christ as you renew your thinking with God's Word. Even so, they're still quite capable of committing sins (plural) (Romans 12:2).

That's why it's so wonderful that God made a way for you and me to be cleansed again, and again, and again.

We don't have to live in condemnation! Any time we stumble into sin, we can be set free from the contamination of it by our Lord and Savior, Jesus Christ—the One who as Revelation 1:5 says, *"loved us, and washed us from our sins in his own blood."*

The word *from* in that Scripture can mean to take something out of context with, out of the control of, out of the influence of, to make pass or go away. According to that, the way Jesus has dealt with your sins has staggering implications! He put them in one place and you in another. He totally separated you from them.

Sins no longer have the legal right to influence you anymore.

Jesus has removed them from you as far as the east is from the west (Psalm 103:12). They cannot control you anymore because their power has been destroyed by His Blood. God has so thoroughly washed you in His Blood, no remainder of those sins can be found in you. Jesus has blotted out the record completely and has taken it away, *"nailing it to his cross"* (Colossians 2:14).

Centuries ago, it was customary, that if accusations were brought against someone, they were written down on paper and nailed to the person's door so everyone could see how bad they had been. Even if a court decided the person wasn't guilty, the handwritten notice wouldn't be removed. It would simply be marked with a big "X" so people would know the defendant had been cleared of the charges.

Imagine how humiliating that would be! You have been pronounced "not guilty," but the ugly things you have been accused of are still there posted to your door for everyone to read.

Praise God, that's not how Jesus handled the record of your sins! He didn't just mark it with an "X." He blotted out all the handwriting on it.

Your record is now totally clean, as if no charge had ever been brought against you. There are no words on it, no sins on it. Jesus erased the itemized wrongs leaving only a clean sheet of paper that says nothing is held against you any longer. He removed all the crimes, all the shame, and all the guilt (Colossians 2:14).

That's what *cleansed* and *washed* means for you. All charges are abolished. There's no trace of sin left. When you believe this, no sin has the power to keep you in its grip. You can overcome and use your authority in Jesus' Name and make that defeated thing bow its knee to you. You can crush your enemy (every sin) into powder—*all because of the Blood* (Psalm 18:42)!

Say what the Blood says about you. Don't agree with the devil. Rejoice over the fact that Jesus has cleansed you through and through. Declare that sin has no dominion over you, and you've been cleared of all guilt through the power of Jesus' Blood. Confess that you are holy and innocent, righteous and pure. Agree with God who loves you and gave His Son just so you could be free!

Prayer and Confession

Precious Father, thank You for making me whole, clean, pure, and holy by the power of the Blood of Jesus. The power in that Blood has brought me life—real life. I can now live free from tormenting sins. You have washed me clean inside and out with Jesus' Blood.

I thank You, Jesus and Holy Spirit, for showing me the truth. I no longer live under sin's dominion, because I can say, "The Blood of Jesus has washed me and cleansed me and made me whole. I am a brand new me. All those old things have truly passed away and everything in my life is brand new!"

Glory to God forevermore, in Jesus' powerful and precious Name I pray!

Proclaim and Decree

I am clean through and through and there's no hand-writing against me.

Other Scriptures to Study

Hebrews 12:9-10

1 John 3:5; 4:10

1 Peter 2:24; 3:18

Day 28

The Good Life—Abundant Life

The thief cometh not, but for to steal, and to kill, and to destroy: I am come that they might have life, and that they might have it more abundantly.

—John 10:10

JESUS came to give you life and to give it to you more abundantly. The word *abundance* can mean more than enough, plenty, over and above. It refers to an overflowing fullness of something good. In other words, to have abundant life means to have *the good life*—and lots of it. Jesus is all about life! The devil is all about death. He wants to do just the opposite of what Jesus has done. He wants to take the good life away from you. He wants to steal what Jesus has given you and bring destruction into your life through sickness, poverty, and sin. How does he plan to do it?

He does it by lies and deception. He is a liar and the father of lies (John 8:44).

The devil will try to tell you that God isn't going to keep the promises He made to you in the Bible. Just like he caused Adam and Eve to believe that God was holding out on them, He will tell you that God will withhold abundant life from you and leave you poor, sick, and defeated (Genesis 3:1-5).

If you believe the devil, he can stop you from receiving and rejoicing over the good life that's yours in Christ Jesus.

He can rob you of the revelation of God's blessings and unjustly enforce on you the curse in Deuteronomy 28:47-48 (AMP):

> Because you did not serve the Lord your God with a heart full of joy and gladness for the abundance of all things... you will therefore serve your enemies whom the Lord sends against you, in hunger and in thirst, in nakedness and in lack of all things; and He will put an iron yoke... on your neck until He has destroyed you.

Those verses aren't supposed to apply to you or me or any other born-again child of God! As believers, we've been redeemed from the curse (Galatians 3:13). Jesus has set us free from every aspect of it and given us His abundant life. He has overcome every negative thing the devil can come up with—and He's done it by the power of His Blood.

Life and death are opposites.

Every time the enemy attacks you with something that's tainted with death, you can oppose it by proclaiming the power in the

THE GOOD LIFE—ABUNDANT LIFE

Blood of Jesus. Faith in Jesus' Blood will override that death-tainted thing and bring life every time!

Don't misunderstand me. I'm not saying physically you'll never die. Unless Jesus comes back within our lifetime, the day will come for all of us when our spirits will leave our bodies. If we're believers, we'll depart this earth to be with the Lord. When that happens, our bodies will die, but not permanently! Because Jesus conquered physical death when He rose from the dead. Ultimately, even our physical bodies will be raised up and glorified to live for eternity with Him (1 Corinthians 15:52).

In the end, we win no matter what!

Life is more powerful than death. Life always triumphs. Through the Blood of the cross, because of His victory over death, life is assured, and we can enjoy it in abundance not only in the ages to come but right now.

Actually, because there is life and resurrection power in Jesus' Blood, it can resurrect things in your life that might already seem to be dead. For instance, maybe you have dreams that have died or maybe you have a body part that's stopped functioning. Don't give up and say, "It's over."

You have resurrection power inside you because of the Blood!

As Romans 8:11 says,

The Spirit of God, who raised Jesus from the dead, lives in you. And just as God raised Christ Jesus from the dead, he will give life to your mortal bodies by this same Spirit living within you.

—Romans 8:11 NLT

Think of it! By the Blood of Jesus and the power of the Holy Spirit, you can be quickened and made abundantly alive in every way.

When you address any situation in your life by speaking in faith about what the Blood has done and is doing, you are speaking the overflowing fullness of God and the power of the Holy Spirit into that situation. You are turning the situation around by releasing into it an abundance of divine life.

Abundant life may not mean living in a mansion with millions of dollars in the bank.

It does mean you will have what you need and more so you can be a blessing to your family with enough to bless others also. You don't live on barely-get-along street anymore. You have everything you need for life and godliness, plus you get to go to Heaven too (2 Peter 1:3)! And the streets are made out of gold up there! That's abundance!

Precious believer, you can live the good life Jesus came to give you. You can overcome lack, poverty, sickness, and sin by applying

His Blood to everything that concerns you. You can be like those in Revelation 12:11 who *"overcame him* [the devil] *by the blood of the Lamb, and by the word of their testimony."*

Your enemy has been defeated. Now enforce his defeat in your life by declaring the power of the Blood.

Prayer and Confession

My Father, I truly believe there's life in the Blood of Jesus. I apply that Blood, **that life,** *to myself, my family, friends, and everything that concerns me right now. I believe everything the Blood of Jesus touches turns to life with abundance. I believe You want me to have abundance so I can be blessed and be a blessing to others. I believe You don't want me to live in lack.*

I believe I receive right now, today, this minute, abundance through the Blood of Jesus Christ, through the power of His cross, by the power of the Holy Spirit. I am being made alive inside right now. I am alive to this truth, that I am living in abundance! Thank You, Lord, and Holy Spirit, for opening my eyes to this revelation.

Praise Your Holy Name, I'm free. I'm free. I'm free from lack, sin, sickness, and poverty by the power of the Blood of Jesus. I have life in me now. That life is bringing abundance into everything that concerns me. In Jesus' Name I pray.

Proclaim and Decree

I am living the abundant life.

Other Scriptures to Study

Matthew 25:29

John 6:53-54

2 Corinthians 8:14

Ephesians 3:19-20

Day 29

The Real You

*For we are God's [own] handiwork (His workmanship),
recreated in Christ Jesus, [born anew] that we may do those
good works which God predestined (planned beforehand)
for us [taking paths which He prepared ahead of time],
that we should walk in them [living the good life which He
prearranged and made ready for us to live].*

—Ephesians 2:10 AMPC

NO matter how insignificant the devil might try to make you feel at times, you are a very important person. You have a divinely appointed destiny and purpose.

Your destiny is *who you are*. Your purpose is *what you do* because of who you are.

They were both established by God before the foundation of the earth. He didn't just throw them together the day you were born. He knew you before you were formed in your mother's womb (Jeremiah 1:5). His plans for your life existed eons ago.

The Bible confirms it again and again. Before you ever knew God, before you ever believed the Gospel and received Jesus as the

Lord of your life, He made good plans for your future (Jeremiah 29:11). He designed an exquisite destiny and fulfilling purpose for you.

Like all human beings, you sensed that was true even as a child. You may have wanted to be a police officer or a teacher one day, and a doctor or a pilot the next. Trying to find out the truth of who you were, you imagined yourself in different roles hoping to identify what you were supposed to do.

You knew even back then, even though you may have forgotten it over the years, that you aren't just a biological accident. You exist for a reason. You were born on purpose for a purpose. It's not just a natural, earthly purpose either. It's great because it's God-ordained and eternal.

Ecclesiastes 3:11 says it this way: God has put eternity in our hearts.

That's why none of us can be satisfied just puttering around on the earth doing ordinary, natural things. We were made for something higher. We are God's workmanship created for His purposes (Ephesians 2:10).

The Old Testament patriarch, Joseph, whose story is found in the book of Genesis, discovered this truth when he was just a teenager. Through a God-given dream, he got a revelation of his divine destiny and purpose. Most likely, Joseph initially expected to fulfill them with ease. But that's not what happened.

Problems soon surfaced in his life. He was hated by his brothers and sold into slavery. He was deceived, insulted, slandered, and unjustly imprisoned.

None of those obstacles could stop Joseph's progress! He always rose to the top. He prospered even as a slave. When imprisoned, God continued to work with him until he became who God created him to be and did what he was born to do. What was Joseph's secret?

First, he continued believing what God had said about him regardless of how desperately the devil tried to refute it. Second, he put the *who* before the *doing*. He took the time to let God develop his character and establish his identity on the inside. When the time came for him to do the big things he was called to do, because he knew who he was, the *doing* was easier for him.

Some Christians don't exercise that kind of patience. They rush into doing without paying much attention to being. Because they don't take the time to discover their real, God-established identity, they wind up trying to be someone they're not and trying to accomplish things God never called them to do.

They remind me of people I see on the road sometimes who are trying to use their car as if it were a truck. They pull out of the lumber yard with boards tied to the roof, sticking out of the trunk and the windows on both sides. Those people may eventually get where they're going, but it'll be a frustrating and painful journey. What's more, if they keep doing that kind of thing, they're going to mess up their car big time!

Much the same thing is true when it comes to your God-given purpose.

You'll mess yourself up if you ignore who you are in Christ and follow your own natural ambitions. Coming up with your own plan and trying to get God to bless it will only cause exhaustion and frustration. I've done it and I know this to be true!

So, don't do it!

Instead, make it your very first priority to find out from God's written Word who you really are.

Learn to see yourself as God describes you in the Bible.

+ Redeemed by Jesus' own Blood according to the riches of His Grace (Ephesians 1:7)
+ Born of God's Spirit (John 3:5)
+ Able to do all things through Christ who strengthens you (Philippians 4:13)
+ With an anointing from the Holy Spirit (1 John 2:20)

The revelation of your true identity is waiting for you in the Bible.

Go after it! Stop listening to what everyone else says about who you are and what you should do. Receive the revelation of what your Father in Heaven has said about it.

Once you begin to understand your real identity, your struggles and frustrations will begin to fade. God's Grace will be activated in your life. Living out of *who* He has made you to be, you'll be able to *do* what He has designed you to do. You'll access God's power and make a huge difference in this world.

- Your life will count for something wonderful and awesome.
- You will have true significance.
- You truly will be living instead of just existing from day to day.
- You will make a mark in this world that will be rewarding here and in Heaven.
- You can live your life on purpose, fulfilling your destiny and purpose.

Prayer and Confession

Father, thank You for helping me to know who I am as Your Blood-bought, Blood-washed child. Thank You for helping me find my significance in You.

You created me for a reason. You've given me a destiny and purpose in this life and called me to be a blessing to humanity. I am somebody. I'm not an accident. I was born on purpose and for a purpose. You had my life all laid out for me before I was born. You even knew my name. You've given me a reason to live and a specific purpose to fulfill.

I embrace all you have for me. Help me to live to my fullest potential in Jesus Christ, my Lord and Savior. Thank You for revealing to me who I am and whose I

am. Thank you for blessing me with Your love, accep-
tance, grace, and mercy as I complete what You've put
in my hands to do. I praise Your Holy Name, Jesus.

Proclaim and Decree

I am important. I am who I am.

Other Scriptures to Study

Exodus 33:12

Isaiah 45:4; 62:2

Jeremiah 1:5

Day 30

Free to Fulfill Your Destiny

If ye continue in my word, then are ye my disciples indeed;
and ye shall know the truth, and the truth shall make you
free.

—John 8:31-32

YOUR destiny isn't just a goal you reach. It's not a physical destination, a place where you arrive and then stop. Like the horizon, your destiny is out in front of you. It's something you continually move toward. It's a journey you are on in this life.

So, let me ask you today. Are you moving in the right direction?

The answer to that question depends on whether or not you have a clear sense of your spiritual identity. Since your destiny is *who you are* and your purpose is *what you do because of who you are*, if you're uncertain about your identity, the devil can easily distract you and get you off course. He can trick you into taking discouraging detours by convincing you to do things that might be good but aren't a part of God's plan for you.

It happens to people all the time—committed, willing, dedicated Christians work diligently in churches and ministries out of a sense of obligation. They want with all their heart to do something for God. But since what they're doing isn't in line with who they are, they fail to experience the deep satisfaction that comes with fulfilling God's perfect plan. Instead, they just get weary and end up producing very disappointing results, because God didn't call them or equip them to do that particular job.

Don't let that happen to you.

Discover the true joy of the Christian life by letting your *do* flow naturally out of your *who!* Find out the truth about your identity and let that truth make you free.

Jesus paid a high price for you to live in that kind of freedom. First, He bought it for you with His precious Blood. Then He cleansed you with that Blood so the Holy Spirit could come to live inside you and be your teacher.

The Holy Spirit will reveal to you everything you need to know about your God-ordained destiny and purpose. He will quicken the written Word to you and show you what it says about who you are in Christ. He will speak to your heart and talk to you personally about God's specific plan for you. He'll strengthen and guide you so that you can be the person you were born again to be.

As I've already mentioned, the devil will do everything he can to hinder this process. He'll try to convince you that you can't hear the Holy Spirit's Voice. He'll try to keep the truth away from you by talking you out of spending time in the Word and prayer.

The enemy knows if he can rob you of the revelation of your spiritual identity—and the authority that accompanies it—he can absolutely stop you or get you sidetracked. Then he can prevent you from finding your God-given destiny on this earth. He can keep you so off balance and insecure, you won't have the courage to stand against him.

Remember this: the devil's entire program is aimed at preventing you from knowing who you are. His goal is to keep you going around in circles, repeating past patterns and acting like who he says you are instead of who God has *made* you to be.

That's what happened to Jacob in the Old Testament in Genesis. Read his story. You will be amazed at how things unfolded for him, but in the end, he won.

His name means *supplanter* or "one who wants to take what belongs to somebody else by scheming or force." He spent many years living out that identity. As a young man, he took the blessing that belonged to his brother, Esau, through an act of deceit. He had to leave his homeland because Esau was so angry that he wanted to kill him.

Eventually, Jacob got tired of running and decided to go home despite the danger. On the way, God spoke to him and gave him a new identity:

> *Thy name shall be called no more Jacob, but Israel: for as a prince hast thou power with God and with men, and hast prevailed.*
>
> —Genesis 32:28

Because Jacob received his new name by faith and believed what God said about him, he was able to make things right with his brother and uncle. He exchanged war for peace, stopped running in fear, and experienced favor with God and man (Genesis 33:3-4).

It's amazing what a new name can do! Through the Blood of Jesus, you've been given a new name. The Blood says your name is:

- Beloved of God (Romans 1:7)
- More than a conqueror (Romans 8:37)
- Joint heir with Christ (Romans 8:17)
- Rich (2 Corinthians 8:9)
- Healed (1 Peter 2:24)
- Righteous (2 Corinthians 5:21)

Through the Blood of Jesus, you have the power to become the successful person God wants you to be. By faith in the Blood, you can *thrive*, not just *survive!* You can turn out like the man in the Bible named Jabez. Although his name meant *sorrow* or *pain*, he cried out to God and received another identity. He prayed and said:

> *"Oh, that You would bless me indeed, and enlarge my territory, that Your hand would be with me, and that You would keep me from evil, that I may not cause pain!" So God granted him what he requested.*
>
> **—1 Chronicles 4:10 NKJV**

Because you're in Christ, you already have a greater identity than Jabez ever dreamed of. You've been born again with a glorious destiny. God has wonderful things for you to do.

You have been created to know your God, *"be strong, and carry out great exploits"* for the Lord and His Kingdom (Daniel 11:32 NKJV).

Allow the Blood of Jesus to wash away every trace of your old, negative identity so you can begin to live as who you truly are. Old things have passed away and it's time for the *new you!* Step up and take your place in God alongside the Bible heroes of the past who, despite their ordinary beginnings, went on to accomplish extraordinary things. Dare to be like…

- Moses—a basket case who led the nation of Israel out of Egyptian bondage.

- David—a humble shepherd turned fugitive, who hid in caves to save his life and then became the greatest king of Israel.

- Jesus—born in a stable and became the King and Savior of the whole world.

Now, what about you? Who are you? How can you change a whole nation? How can you change the whole world?

Go ye into all the world, tell them about Jesus and your new life!

God has made you an original—*don't let the world, anything, or anyone turn you into a copy!*

> [Jesus said,] *If the Son therefore shall make you free, ye shall be free indeed.*
>
> —John 8:36

That means you're free to move toward your destiny.

You're free to be a real, victorious, overcoming heir of the living God.

Hold on to that freedom and don't ever go back into the devil's bondage again. The whole creation is waiting to see the real you (Romans 8:19). Come on, we are waiting on you! We need you!

Prayer and Confession

Precious Heavenly Father, I am so glad You made me an original. I refuse to allow anything to make me a copy. There is something I can do that no one else can do. You have made me unique, an individual, one of a kind, so I can fulfill my portion in Your Kingdom.

*Thank You for teaching me **who** I am so I can **do** what I'm supposed to do and experience the satisfaction in this life of knowing that I am working with You. Help me to see the bigger picture of life instead of just existing day to day.*

*I believe the power in the Blood of Jesus is setting me free—**free to be me**. I believe the enemy cannot stop me because I have the Blood working for me, in me, through me and on my behalf. I am an overcomer. I am protected. I am set free. I know the truth now about myself.*

I love You because You first loved me. You are so wonderful to care about me like You do, Father. I'm so thankful for Jesus who made all this possible just for me. Thank You for the Holy Spirit working in me to reveal truth about me. I love You, Lord, and I am grateful for Your love, Your help, and the Blood of Jesus that has set me free. I am free indeed in Jesus' Name!

Proclaim and Decree

I am "me" created in the image of Christ. I will fulfill my destiny and purpose.

Other Scriptures to Study

Isaiah 61; 58:6

Romans 6:18, 22

Ephesians 2:10

1 Corinthians 7:22

Day 31

The Power of His Blood

But ye are come...to Jesus the mediator of the new covenant, and to the blood of sprinkling, that speaketh better things than that of Abel.

—Hebrews 12:22, 24

There is much more in the written Word of God for you to read, study, hear and understand about the power of the Blood. In this book we've only covered a fraction of it. Yet even so, the truths on these pages are enough to change your life. Just think of what you've seen in the past 30 days! You've learned that...

1. The Blood of Jesus speaks "Mercy."

It speaks *for* you, *to* you and *against* your enemy, the devil. Just as Abel's blood cried out from the ground when he was murdered by his brother, Jesus' Blood cried out when it ran from His body, down the cross and into the ground on the day He was crucified. But instead of calling for vengeance as Abel's blood did, Jesus' Blood spoke—and still speaks *better things!* It speaks *Mercy.* It cries out for your forgiveness and redemption. Because the Voice of Jesus' Blood is powerful and full of authority and speaking on your behalf today, you can come boldly to the Throne of Grace to obtain mercy and find grace to help in every time of need (Hebrews 4:16).

2. Jesus' Life is in His Blood.

The moment you made Jesus your Lord and received the saving gift of His Blood, you received His very life. You were born again. The sin nature you had inherited from Adam, which had the seed of spiritual death in it, was done away with. You received a new nature, the very nature of God, and became a brand-new creature. Old things passed away and all things became new (2 Corinthians 5:17). Because the life is in the blood (Leviticus 17:11), you can now experience the life of Jesus in every area. You can speak His life over your mind, emotions, relationships, body and circumstances just by declaring the power of His Blood!

3. The Blood of Jesus has set you free from the power of sin.

Because the Blood has wiped out the fallen sinful nature that was in you and replaced it with the nature of God, you are free from the power of sin. You no longer need to live as a slave to the temptations of the flesh and the devil. Instead, you can defeat them! As Romans 6:14 says, *"Sin shall not have dominion over you: for you are not under law but under grace"* (NKJV).

The more of God's Grace you reach out and receive, the more you will be able to exercise your authority over sin and live like one who has truly been set free!

4. Because of the Blood you can enjoy true fellowship with God.

Before you were born again, sin stood as a barrier between you and the Father. Because He was righteous and you were sinful, you couldn't draw near to Him. Now things have changed! You have boldness to enter the heavenly Holy of Holies by the Blood of Jesus. You can draw near to God with a true heart in full assurance of faith (Hebrews 10:19, 22). Your heart and your conscience have been purified by Jesus' Blood, so you can fellowship freely with the Father, with Jesus and with the Holy Spirit (1 John 1:3, 7; 2 Corinthians 13:14). You can enjoy a very real and close relationship with God.

5. You are cleansed and washed by the Blood.

According to Revelation 1:5,

Jesus Christ, who is the faithful witness, and the first begotten of the dead, and the prince of the kings of the earth.

He is the One *"who loved us and washed us from our sins in his own blood."* When Jesus washed you, He washed you completely. Every part of you—spirit, soul, and body—has been cleansed through the power of His Blood. Any time you happen to stumble and commit a sin, you can always receive a fresh *power wash* by acting on 1 John 1:9:

If we confess our sins, he is faithful and just to forgive us our sins, and to cleanse us from all unrighteousness.

6. The Blood of Jesus has redeemed you from the curse.

The curse, which came on the earth through sin and the work of the devil, is the source of every bad thing on earth. It produces nothing but sickness, poverty, defeat, and destruction. Nobody wants to live under the curse. Thank God, as a believer you don't have to. You've been delivered from it (Galatians 3:13). You've been redeemed not with:

> ...*corruptible things, as silver and gold...but with the precious Blood of Christ, as of a lamb without blemish and without spot.*
>
> —1 Peter 1:18-19

Because of the Blood, the curse has no power over you. You've been loosed from the devil's hold. You've been freed from any and all curses in every area of life! The Bible says,

> *Let the redeemed of the Lord say so, whom he hath redeemed from the hand of the enemy.*
>
> —Psalm 107:2

When any part of the curse tries to attach itself to you, open your mouth and declare, "I am redeemed!"

7. Through the Blood you are justified.

In an earthly court of law, to be justified means to be declared not guilty. But in the court of Heaven it means much more. It means you've been *made innocent*. It means the charges against you have not just been dropped, but they've been obliterated. Jesus blotted them out completely with His Blood. In the eyes of God, there is no case pending against you. Jesus has totally erased all your sins. It's as if they never existed.

> *Much more then, being now justified by his blood, we shall be saved from wrath through him.*
>
> —Romans 5:9

Allow yourself to experience that justification by giving voice to what Jesus did for you. When accusing voices from your past condemn you, talk back to them. Say, "Jesus' Blood has made me innocent. I'm not guilty. I am justified." Give voice to the Blood loudly in your life. Let it speak for you and to the devil on your behalf.

8. Because of the Blood, you have peace with God.

In the Old Testament, Jesus is called "the Prince of Peace" (Isaiah 9:6). The Hebrew word for peace, which is *shalom*, refers to being made whole with nothing missing and nothing broken. That's what the Blood of Jesus has done for you! It's made you whole. It's put all the pieces of your once-broken life back together again. The wall of sin that once separated you from God has been removed and you have been united with Him (Colossians 1:20; Romans 5:1). Because you now have peace with God, you can have peace with others. You can say what the Blood says to the turbulent thoughts and emotions that try to overwhelm you. You can speak to tumultuous circumstances in your life and say, "Peace, be still!"

9. The Blood of Jesus has provided you with an everlasting Covenant.

You can experience true spiritual security because you have a relationship with God that has no end. Your Covenant with Him will remain in force and never be interrupted through all of eternity. Because Jesus ratified it with His own Blood, you can't mess it up. When you fail, the Blood provides mercy for your failure. It cleanses you and keeps the Covenant intact. This should bring you much comfort. It's wonderful to know that regardless of mistakes and failures, God will never give up on you. He started this work of faith in you and He will finish it (Philippians 1:6)! He will, through the Blood of the everlasting Covenant:

> ...make you perfect in every good work to do his will, working in you that which is wellpleasing in his sight, through Jesus Christ; to whom be glory for ever and ever.
>
> —Hebrews 13:20-21

10. The Blood provides the riches of His Grace.

Grace is the power to change and overcome sin. Mercy is God's power to forgive sins. He is rich in Grace and gives Grace to you abundantly. Ephesians 2:7 teaches us:

> That in the ages to come he might shew the exceeding riches of his grace in his kindness toward us through Christ Jesus.

This richness of His Grace is because of His Blood. Look at this:

whom we have redemption through his blood, the for-
giveness of sins, according to the riches of his grace.

—Ephesians 1:7

The power of Grace is absolutely amazing. It saves but also changes everything about us that needs it, all because of the Blood. You can change! All because God is "rich" in Grace and He gives it to you liberally!

11. You are forgiven so that you can forgive and live a holy life.

You can forgive because you have been forgiven. You have the power inside yourself to forgive others. Also, you can forgive yourself! Forgiveness is the way to be free. Because you are forgiven, you can live a holy life set apart for the Master's service. It feels so good to know that He has *made* you righteous, so you don't have to be concerned all the time about being wrong. The Blood is continually washing, sanctifying, and making you clean.

12. Every drop of Jesus' Blood was poured out for you.

His Blood was poured out in the Garden, where Jesus sweated great drops of Blood and said to God, "Thy will be done," so that your will could be redeemed and you would have the strength to overcome like He did and say, "Thy will be done in my life too."

Blood poured out of His back as He submitted to the Roman whips and took stripes so that you could be healed (1 Peter 2:24).

Jesus' Blood poured from His head when He wore the crown of thorns so that all your yesterdays of sorrow, mourning, and brokenness could be replaced with a crown of life.

His Blood poured from His hands and feet when He allowed them to be pierced with nails so that your walk with God (your conduct) could be pure and holy, your feet could be shod with peace, and you could do the good works God called you to do.

It poured from His side, which was pierced so that you could be delivered from the thorns in your side of life's hardest trials and live in total liberty.

Think of it! Anything the devil could try to hold against you, anything he could accuse you of, has been taken care of by the power of the Blood of Jesus. Through the Blood, you've been made more than a conqueror. You can exercise authority over all power of the enemy (Luke 10:19). *You always win and never lose.* The devil always loses and never wins because Jesus has made you triumphant!

Prayer and Confession

Father, please open my eyes so that I can understand all that Jesus has done for me. Flood my mind with the light and truth of the revelation of who I truly am through the power of His Blood (Ephesians 1:17-20; 2:4-22).

Lord, how can I ever thank You enough for the wonderful gift of that Blood? I worship and honor You for it. I'm so glad You had a plan for me—and for all mankind—before the foundation of the world. It's truly the best plan ever! Through the Blood of Jesus, You have made us winners in this life and in the life to come.

Thank You for loving me, Father. Thank You for understanding. Thank You that my name is written in the Lamb's Book of Life by His Blood. Thank You, Lord, thank You.

Proclaim and Decree

I am *loved!*

Other Scriptures to Study

John 19:34

Romans 3:24

Acts 26:18

Ephesians 2:10

2 Thessalonians 1:12

Acknowledgments

I WOULD like to acknowledge my amazing family. I feel like I have the most awesome family in the world. Each one is uniquely special and deeply treasured; they are the sunshine of my life. My children, grandchildren, and great-grandchildren have brought me joy unspeakable. They are all dedicated to and serving the Lord with their whole heart. What a blessing indeed! I am eternally grateful and thankful to the Lord for the precious family He has given me.

I've had the most amazing prayer partners and friends who have stayed beside me through all these years to see this book become a reality. There are way too many to name, but here are a few: Mary Ann Wilson for her research and contribution, Annie Grace, Darlene C., Sammie, Darlene L., Shirley, Brenda, Gina L., Debbi, Janet, Lynn, Trudy, Christa, Kyle, Roberta, and so many more. I am truly blessed to be surrounded by such dedicated and committed people of God, of like precious faith who love the Lord and me.

About Ginger Ziegler

G INGER ZIEGLER has been in full-time
ministry since 1981. She has assisted in
the foundation of multiple churches, Bible
schools, started several leadership/training schools,
and prison ministry.

Ginger has fulfilled the office of pastor, teacher, and
overseer of many other functions. She has preached in
several foreign countries doing mission work, including ministers' conferences.

She worked for Kenneth Copeland Ministries,
Calvary Cathedral, and other ministries and churches
before starting Embracing His Grace in 1991. Her
heart's desire is for people to know the love of God
in a personal way so they can fulfill their destiny and
purpose in life.

For more books and updates:

Ginger Ziegler Ministries
Embracing His Grace
PO Box 163555
Fort Worth, TX 76161

 https://gingerziegler.com

 staff@embracinghisgrace.org

 facebook.com/GingerZieglerEHG

 twitter.com/Ginger_Ziegler

 instagram.com/GingerZieglerEHG

 youtube.com/GingerZiegler

Equipping Believers to Walk in the Abundant Life
John 10:10b

Connect with us on

Facebook @ HarrisonHousePublishers

and Instagram @ HarrisonHousePublishing

so you can stay up to date with news

about our books and our authors.

Visit us at **www.harrisonhouse.com**

Made in the USA
Coppell, TX
04 May 2024

32030419R00115